GARDENS *of* *the* RIVIERA

GARDENS *of the* RIVIERA

— • —

VIVIAN RUSSELL

LITTLE, BROWN AND COMPANY
Boston New York Toronto London

To my parents Petro and Harvey Jolly

with happy memories of our garden in Cap Ferrat which many years later inspired this book.

A LITTLE, BROWN BOOK

COPYRIGHT © 1993 VIVIAN RUSSELL
THE MORAL RIGHT OF THE AUTHOR HAS BEEN ASSERTED

FIRST PUBLISHED IN GREAT BRITAIN IN 1993 BY LITTLE, BROWN AND COMPANY

ISBN 0-316-90556-9

A CIP CATALOGUE RECORD FOR THIS BOOK IS AVAILABLE FROM THE BRITISH LIBRARY

DESIGNED BY DAVID FORDHAM
TYPESET BY SX COMPOSING
PRINTED AND BOUND IN ITALY BY GRAPHICOM SRL, VICENZA

LITTLE, BROWN AND COMPANY (UK) LTD
165 GREAT DOVER STREET
LONDON SE1 4YA

ACKNOWLEDGEMENTS

I HAVE WIDENED THE BORDERS OF THE RIVIERA to include three gardens in Provence, and the Alpine Garden of the Lautaret. Two seminal Riviera gardens, one of which is Chèvre d'Or, are sadly absent for personal and security reasons.

A book about gardeners and their gardens would not be possible without the help and tacit trust of the gardeners themselves and I must thank each and every garden owner and director who provided information and photographs. Sir Hanmer and Lady Hanbury, Pier Giorgio Campodonico, Professor Paula Profumo of La Mortola; Guido Piacenza of Boccanegra; William Waterfield and Nancy Tennant on Clos du Peyronnet; Anne and Antony Norman of Château de la Garoupe; Pippa Irwin, Renée Iliffe and Bruno Goris on Villa Roquebrune; René Ghiglione and Ariane Van der Elst; Nicole de Vésian at La Louve; Claus Scheinert and Tom Parr at La Casella; Piero and Henriette Chiesa at Château de Vignal; Jane Harvey at Villa Noailles; Pierre Quillier at Parc St Bernard; Bruno Goris at l'Oustau dei Baelea; Lulu de Waldner at Jas Crema; Cecile Chancel at Val Joanis; Dr Marcel Kroenlein from the Jardin Exotique de Monte Carlo; the Duc de Clarens from Château de Beauregard; Pierre Deval and his daughter Francine from Orves; Mlle Sekakini from Parc Borely de Marseilles; Professor Gerard Cadel of the Jardin Alpin du Lautaret; Professor Yves Monnier from Val Rahmeh; Jean Hubert Gilson from the town of Menton to whom Serre de la Madone and Fontana Rosa now belong. Consistently helpful and generous with his expertise has been Bruno Goris, and special thanks go to William Waterfield, Nicole de Vesian, and Lulu de Waldner.

For help in bringing the gardens to life I am grateful to Henri Perrot and his daughter, and to Roy Lancaster, a colleague of the Vicomte de Noailles. Invaluable was Pierre Schneider's interview with Charles de Noailles in American *Vogue* and my thanks for his permission to quote at length from it. To Pippa Irwin and Lady Renée Iliffe for their thoughts and affection for Norah Warre; James Russell who knew both Mrs Warre and Lawrence Johnston was a great help. To Freddie Braun for his amusing descriptions of Lawrence Johnston's malevolent parrot and the pugnacious Ibañez; to Marguerite, Raymond and Hubert Arsento for an absorbing afternoon spent talking about Maybud Campbell.

Audrey Le Lievre's evocative biography of Ellen Willmott was a godsend and Mary Blume's amusing and quirky book *Côte d'Azur – Inventing the French Riviera* provided many artistic and literary leads which I followed with the efficient help of A & R Booksearch and Chris Hurley at the London Library. Thanks also due to my father Harvey Jolly who scoured the libraries of Paris, and to Marcel Gaucher for the correspondence that ensued. For the material on Edith Wharton's friendship with Lawrence Johnston and Charles de Noailles and photographs of Ste Claire, I am indebted to Rebecca Cape from Indiana University's Lilly Library. My thanks also go to Yale's Beinecke Library for the correspondence between Wharton and Beatrix Farrand. No garden book is ever begun or finished without the help of the Royal Horticultural Society, Lindley Library, who lent us photographs of La Mortola.

Warmest thanks to the team at Little Brown, especially my editorial director Vivien Bowler; to copy editor Steve Dobell for his sensitivity; to indexer Penny David for her assiduity, and to designer David Fordham for choosing the more unusual shots and giving us such an elegant book. To the unflappable Helen Parker, a diplomatic go-between and the recipient of frantic messages delivered from a creaking French phonebox. And to editor Janet Ravenscroft of whom infinite patience is demanded and who receives all the anxiety and none of the glory.

On the domestic front, my thanks go to Peter Barton who looked after my children during the photography and after all of us during the writing and who also proof read and ironed out the first draft. To Louisa Jones for her cheerful faxes and Colette Gehu always on the end of the phone. And finally, thank you Molly and Rupert, purveyors of endless cups of tea for a seemingly never ending book. I hope I haven't put you off publishing!

All the colour photographs in this book were taken with a Leica R5 camera and lenses and shot on Fuji Velvia film, 50 ASA. Additional picture credits: p8 Alan Clark; p106 Charles de la Haye Jousselin; p47 Country Life/IPC magazines; p11, p78 The Hulton Deutsch Collection; p9 Magnum Photos Ltd; p30 Yves Monnier; p14 Musée Colette; p9 Musée Renoir; p13 Syndication International; p16 Edmund Uher; p34 Andriano Viale; p19 Ville de Menton. Whilst every effort has been made to trace copyright holders, this has proved impossible in some cases and copyright owners are invited to contact the publishers.

CONTENTS

———•———

OPPOSITE TITLE PAGE: THE PARTERRE AT CHATEAU DE
GOURDON.
FRONT COVER: THE NEW GARDEN AT CHATEAU DE LA
GAROUPE, DESIGNED BY ANTONY NORMAN.
BACK COVER: THE POTAGER AT VAL JOANIS.

Introduction

PARADISE FOUND, PARADISE LOST

———•———

T HE STORY OF GARDENERS AND THEIR GARDENS ON THE Riviera is a tale of many love affairs beginning roughly a hundred and fifty years ago. Seduced by its golden light, the warmth, and fragrant air that quickened the senses and kindled their imaginations, intoxicated by the horticultural raptures they foresaw, these gardeners plunged headlong into their *petite aventure* going to any lengths and sometimes any extravagance to consummate it.

Explorers, expatriates, exiles, life wanderers, they flew in like migrating birds seeking the sun – which in many cases had not shone upon their childhoods – and alighted in this haven to feather happier nests. This unspoiled virginal paradise welcomed everybody; its salutary climate offered solace to the ill and ailing, and to the northern gardener provided the answer to a prayer. It attracted the prosaic, the seedy and shady, as well as extraordinary men and women for whom it was an intensely creative and productive experience. They were curious, energetic, purposeful and persevering and, bound by a genuine love of visual beauty, they stamped their tastes, conceits and personalities upon the gardens they created.

No other stretch of coast can claim to have captured the imaginations and the hearts of such an eclectic array of talent, drawn from many disciplines, who applied their fertile wits to a frequently infertile soil. They brought their artistry as writers and painters, and expertise as botanists, plantsmen, plant hunters and landscape gardeners to bear upon their chosen spots, while with their varied culture and experience they also interacted socially with each other. From England came Lawrence Johnston, Lady Aberconway, Ellen Willmott and Harold Peto, the creators of Hidcote, Bodnant, Warley Place and Ilford Manor; from America came Edith Wharton, the first woman Pulitzer prize winner and author of *Italian Villas and Their Gardens*. Among them were accomplished botanists such as Gustave Thuret and Daniel Hanbury, who had already made important contributions in their fields; sexual exiles like Somerset Maugham, political exiles like Blasco Ibañez. Free from cultural and social restraints, they made gardens as showplaces, gardens as plantsmen's paradises; botanical or ideological gardens; and gardens in which they simply perfected the art of living.

THE SHELL OF FONTANA ROSA'S LIBRARY AND CINEMA, ITS CRUMBLING COLUMNS CONTRASTING WITH THE STURDY TRUNK OF THE CANARY PALM. NATURE, AS EVER, IS TRIUMPHANT.

To those who were creative, the place demanded that they respond to it creatively. The painters used it as inspiration and looked to the orchards, olive groves, cypresses and pine trees which repeat themselves in endless variations across the landscape, giving it character and definition. In gardens and on boulevards, a palm is no longer just a palm, but Matisse's stylized palm, brilliantly heightened; so it is with Van Gogh's cypresses and olives, his irises and sunflowers because, in a way, he first 'saw' them here. It did not matter to the painters if their plants and trees were rare, native or exotic, the flowers scarlet or puce, as long as the picture was balanced within itself and the colours as strong and vibrant as the light. In choosing to paint the trees and flowers that they did, the painters gave the Riviera its identity. The philodendron is a houseplant common the world over, but by virtue of being used in so many different ways by Matisse, it has come to symbolize this particular painter's affinity with the Côte d'Azur. By contrast, whole forests of holm oaks proliferate there, but who instantly associates the holm oak with the Riviera? We think instead of the cypress, the palm and the pine.

The artists who came to the Riviera always changed their style completely, becoming bolder, more vibrant, more colourful, as they tried to express some of the intoxication induced by the sensuality all around them – flowers, trees, landscape, scents – evoking with a paintbrush that which a gardener makes real with a spade.

Artists make you see the beauty of things. Kenneth Clark once remarked that no one ever thought the rocky hills of Provence beautiful until Cézanne painted them. Described by Matisse as the 'father of us all', Cézanne was the Pied Piper of Provence. The only native among the Impressionists, he brought Monet and Renoir to the Riviera in search of new inspiration. 'It is so clear, so luminous, like swimming in blue air, it's frightening' wrote Monet from Antibes in 1888. In a state of exultation he painted forty canvases in nine months, but never painted there again.

The sensuality of Provence possessed Van Gogh. 'Dreaming of the sun and of love and gaiety' he arrived in 1888 to what he called 'the land of blue tones and gay colours' and during the last three years of his life he threw himself into it, body and soul. It meant fighting off mosquitos, and battling against the infuriating mistral, his canvas 'shaking all the time' and covered in dust. For the first two months after his arrival he was permanently 'drunk' on orchards, then wild flowers, then harvests, each season bringing new raptures. He wrote begging his brother Theo quickly to send more canvas, more brushes, more paints – for 'nature won't wait' – and describing in detail in his many letters what his subjects were, and in precise detail his use of colour. He perceived ordinary garden plants with a painter's eye: an immense vine, green, purple, yellow, with black and orange branches; or a 'red vineyard, all red like red wine'; oleanders 'raving mad . . . flowering so riotously they may well catch locomotor ataxia'; or the 'funereal' cypresses, which were 'as beautiful of line

HENRI MATISSE
PHOTOGRAPHED IN JUNE 1951
BY CARTIER-BRESSON IN THE
GARDEN OF TERIADE,
PUBLISHER OF *VERVE*.

and proportion as an Egyptian obelisk. It is a splash of black in a sunny landscape.' He followed Pissarro's dictum that one must 'boldly exaggerate the effects of either harmony or discord which colour produces', and as he strained to balance six colours, this serene cypress became a cypress blowing in the mistral. In his fevered fascination for objects in strain, his mind began to work itself into a lyrical delirium and finally he had his first breakdown. He would sit in the courtyard at the hospital in St Rémy amid a profusion of spring flowers, painting. In his last days there he painted violet wild irises, bouquets of roses, olive orchards against many-hued skies, 'painted' he believed 'for the first time in this manner'. He committed suicide in Normandy the following year.

Van Gogh had predicted that the artist of the future would be a 'colourist as has never been'. When Matisse arrived inauspiciously in Nice twenty-five years later with rain pouring down continuously, he was confined to his hotel room, reduced to painting the umbrella in its slop bucket. After two weeks he was ready to leave, but on the morning of his departure the sun shone. He unpacked, and stayed for thirty-five years. Initially, he lived mainly in hotel suites, painting the Battle of the Flowers from his hotel window, and in the public gardens of Nice responding to the *joie de vivre* he felt with bold colours, with which he 'invented' the Mediterranean. Raoul Dufy, a disciple of his, echoed this style in his work, but Matisse became interested in other forms and ideas. After the war he rented a villa near Vence with his son, and began rather obsessively to study the leaves in his garden; recording the different shapes, their distribution upon a branch and how they grew and withered. He and Picasso had used the philodendron as a leitmotif, pulling the shape around, reworking it into endless variations.

Nearby lived the Russian artist Chagall. He visited the Riviera in the 1920s. This cultivated paradise and its light were a revelation to him. He found the countryside around Nice dazzling and used flowers symbolically in his landscapes and still life paintings thereafter. Twenty years later he returned, still in love with the Mediterranean and settled in Vence. Both he and Matisse were watched over and encouraged by Teriade, the French publisher of *Verve*, in whose garden Matisse was wonderfully photographed by Henri Cartier-Bresson.

Unlike Van Gogh, Renoir managed to achieve a perfect balance between his art and his life. Although compelled to paint, he never lost his grip on reality. Following a cycling accident, Renoir developed muscular rheumatism and as he grew older he longed increasingly for the warmth of the sun to relieve the aches and pains which eventually almost paralysed him. During the winter of 1900 he rented a villa outside Grasse whose garden was filled with exotic plants, so exotic that his son Jean began collecting reptiles.

THE PAINTER AUGUSTE RENOIR
IN HIS GARDEN AT LES
COLLETTES. ALTHOUGH
CRIPPLED WITH RHEUMATISM
IN HIS FINAL YEARS, HE
ALWAYS MANAGED TO GRASP A
PAINTBRUSH ONE WAY OR
ANOTHER.

RENOIR'S TRANQUIL OLIVE
GROVE AT LES COLLETTES IS
MUCH VISITED BY LOCALS,
LOVERS, ARTISTS AND
PILGRIMS ALIKE.

In 1907 Les Collettes in Cagnes became his final home, bought as a grand gesture of conservation. He had been living in the nearby village of Le Cannet, and would be taken by horse and victoria into the countryside to look for landscapes to paint. In this way he came across Les Collettes – a small farmhouse surrounded by olives reputed to be over a thousand years old, and others planted by King François the First that had never been cultivated and had grown tall and free. The play of light through the silvery leaves fascinated Renoir, and he often went there to paint. Then came the news that the property was to be sold to a carnation grower from Nice who would cut them all down. Without hesitation Renoir bought it himself. Madame Renoir went to work on the nine acres. 'The olive trees were tended, dug around, watered and pruned just enough for their good, but not too much, for fear of distressing Renoir by their mutilation.' The orange trees were manured, hundreds of tangerine trees planted and two vineyards established. Orange blossoms for the perfumeries of Grasse and olive harvests brought life and activity to an otherwise isolated spot. Madame Renoir also started a vegetable garden and built a hen-house to keep poultry. Flowers, fruit and vegetables were either used in the household, taken to market or brought to Renoir's studio, where they would be painted in vases, and the fruit used for still lifes. The gardeners always had to ask permission to cut the grass or weed the paths. What weeds? Renoir would ask.

Gradually, as Renoir's health deteriorated, his suffering increased.

He became so thin that his pointed bones jabbed at his skin and covered him in sores. Arthritis had seized his joints, his fingers curled and twisted inwards; he was unable even to wipe his nose, but miraculously his eyesight remained sharp, his arm steady.

After Madame Renoir died during the First World War, according to her son Jean, the film maker, 'gloom descended on the household, the garden grew wild'. No longer wanting to paint in the cold perfect light of his large studio, Renoir escaped into the garden having a glass shelter built for himself in order to be amongst the wild roses and the great olive trees with their albescent nuances which were such a solace in his final years. Sitting in a wicker armchair with two poles and always dapper in a white linen hat, he was carried down every morning either to his glass shelter or around the garden 'looking for a landscape'. The Mediterranean morning would unfold in all its glory, the sound of the cicadas, the smell of blossom, of grasses. Underneath the olives in a flower filled meadow, the model would take her position. 'It's intoxicating' he kept repeating. Then he would start to hum. It was under such conditions that he painted 'Les Grandes Baigneuses', which he considered his greatest painting.

On 3 December 1919, confined to his bed with a lung infection, Renoir asked for paints and brushes and spent the morning painting a bunch of anemones brought in from the garden. The cook, Grande Louise, recalls him murmuring, 'I think I am beginning to understand something about it'. By sunset, he was dead.

Cézanne, Monet and Matisse, Winston Churchill said, brought joie de vivre to painting and the 'beauty of their work is instinct with gaiety and floats on sparkling air'. Churchill adored the Riviera and painted there for forty years, a houseguest in some of the choicest villas. In the 1920s he stayed at Lou Seuil, the home of Consuelo Balsan, and was a regular guest of Maxine Elliot, Lord Beaverbrook at Cap d'Ail, and towards the end of his life, at La Pausa, Coco Chanel's villa in Roquebrune.

Chanel had sold La Pausa to Churchill's literary agent, Emery Reves, and Churchill spent many weeks there. 'Pausaland was really a temple of peace,' he wrote after a visit, 'there is not much elsewhere.' He cut a unique and memorable figure standing in front of his easel under an enormous Texan hat and parasol, surrounded by his painting paraphernalia and a full cigar box. Wendy Reves had retained the spirit of Chanel by planting the whole garden with lavender like a 'sea of grey-blue which lapped up to the terrace of the house' wrote Churchill's daughter Mary Soames. With his friend Rab Butler, also an accomplished 'Sunday painter' he spent many congenial hours at La Pausa. They sat back to back – Winston painted a seascape with rocks and pines while Rab painted the mountains behind. Clementine, Winston's wife, did not care for the Riviera. For company Churchill had his little canary, Toby, 'a wonderful little bird', given to him as an eightieth birthday present. It was his constant companion for a number of years, and they went everywhere together – from Chequers to Monte Carlo. When his little friend Toby had finally flown away, Churchill's hearing

WINSTON CHURCHILL RELAXING AT LA MAURESQUE, HOME OF HIS FRIEND SOMERSET MAUGHAM. THEY WERE OFTEN JOINED BY LORD BEAVERBROOK, WHOSE GARDEN CHURCHILL FREQUENTLY PAINTED IN.

had deserted him, and his desire to paint had faded. He would sit in the garden at Cap d'Ail, surrounded by 'light and colour, peace and hope'. When he too had dissolved from the picture and the gardens had disappeared beneath concrete, only the paintings remained. 'The canvas,' he once wrote, 'is the screen between Time and Decrepitude.'

Although the Riviera had always inspired writers, it did not necessarily inspire them to live there. But in the 1920s literary cartels sprang up all along the coast, which Cyril Connolly christened Huxley Point, Castle Wharton and Cape Maugham. Working in what Mary Blume called a 'sunlit balance of industry and pleasure', writers such as Colette, Edith Wharton and Somerset Maugham picked up their pens and with their backs to the view because the beauty was too distracting, wrote novels and described the delights of living in the gardens they had made there.

In diaries, biographies and works of fiction, the gardens ring with life and imagination, not as ends in themselves, but as part of a wider view, and had they not existed, neither would the books have been written. They were made by people who flew their respective flags on foreign soil, creating their ideal world. Villa Mauresque was Maugham's independent island for, as he said himself, he never felt at home anywhere. Blasco Ibañez, exiled from his beloved Valencia, recreated it at Fontana Rosa. Gerald and Sara Murphy, escaping Prohibition and overbearing parents, dedicated Villa America to freedom and original-

AN ECLECTIC MIXTURE OF THE CACTUS CEREUS AND CITRUS TREES IN THE BACKSTREETS OF OLD MENTON.

12

ity. For a Burgundian like Colette, St Tropez was another planet, but by virtue of 'scratching round and round like a dog in a basket' she reclaimed her 'peasant' roots.

Amongst the many consumptives who flocked to Menton, like pilgrims to Lourdes, were Katherine Mansfield and Robert Louis Stevenson, pens sharpened by a sense of impending doom. Katherine Mansfield found that illness suddenly increased her longing for nature a million times: 'Still to smell the white waxy scent that lay upon the jonquil fields and the wild spicy scent of the rosemary growing in little tufts among the red rocks closed to the brim of the sea', which she described as the colour of blue hyacinths or crocuses and delighted in her 'wonderful flashing palms', their trunks 'stubborn and solid, and springing from their tops the stiff green bouquets and among them the blue gum trees, tall and slender with sickle shaped leaves and drooping branches half blue, half violet.'

Robert Louis Stevenson rented a little house high up in Hyères and called it La Solitude. Just above lay Edith Wharton's future home and looking out over a garden of 'roses, aloes, olives and fig-marigolds', his 'Delectable Mountains' in the distance, he wrote *Child's Garden of Verses* and *Black Arrow*. He wished later that he could have ended his days in Hyères, because never had he felt so completely happy since.

King Leopold of Belgium, whose real estate acquisitions included Cap Ferrat and the Congo, swam in his pool in what is now the very private botanical garden, Les Cèdres, with his long white beard tucked into a rubber envelope. Haunted by the idea that he might die without receiving extreme unction, he had built a villa nearby for a retired Roman Catholic bishop. This Moorish style house was the Villa Mauresque and by the time Somerset Maugham acquired it in 1926 it was already a derelict white elephant with acres of terraced garden overrun by weeds. It was bought cheaply, Maugham said, 'because it was so ugly'. The villa became one of the landmarks of the Riviera. People came from all around to see his avocados. He claimed they were the first to be grown in Europe, smuggled in from California as cuttings in a golf bag. Seven years later, when they began to fruit, he harvested three hundred and fifty pounds each year.

SOMERSET MAUGHAM OUTSIDE HIS VILLA, THE GATEPOSTS OF WHICH HE DECORATED WITH THE STYLIZED HAND OF THE PROPHET MOHAMMED'S DAUGHTER FATIMA PAINTED IN RED. HE ALSO STAMPED THE SYMBOL ON THE SPINE OF ALL HIS BOOKS.

'I had never had a garden of my own before,' he wrote, 'and didn't know that the more garden you have the more you want, and the more you do, the more cries out to be done.' There were pines, orange trees, mimosas and aloes in the garden, and a tangle of wild thyme, tarragon and rosemary, which the cook used in his famous vinaigrette.

A few months before war was declared he decided, somewhat perversely, to go ahead with a new bulb garden and ordered twenty thousand bulbs. 'Narcissus, daffodils, clusiana, iris and clilia. My eyes dazzled with the blaze of colour I foresaw. Plenty of arums scattered in various places and these I proposed to transplant.' War was declared, the Italians were coming, the British were advised to leave; the last boat, carrying coal, was about to depart. 'I took a last stroll in my garden, which if I went I should in all probability never see again.' He took a phial of poison with him just in case, and boarded the boat.

He did return after the war and led, he liked to say, a very simple life, reducing his staff from thirteen to five but continuing to entertain a good deal. Summer was reserved for the livelier guests like Harold Nicolson who described it as 'the perfect holiday – heat intense, garden lovely, chair long and cool, a bathing pool there if one wishes to splash, and above all the sense that it is not going on too long . . . I went up and sat alone with Tacitus by the swimming pool surrounded by great massifs of red and white oleanders. I stayed there until the red oleanders became invisible and only the white oleanders shone in the moon.' The storm of 1956 toppled two hundred and sixty of Maugham's trees. 'I never knew I had so many' he wrote.

Someone who dreaded being placed next to Maugham at a dinner party was Countess Russell, Elizabeth von Arnim, the author of *Elizabeth and Her German Garden*. She came quite late to the Riviera through the fervent desire of her friend Bridget Guinness, who so wanted her company that she built Elizabeth a house on her own property, Notre Dame de Vie (later bought by Picasso). She called it L'Enchantement, after Elizabeth's book, *The Enchanted April*. The house proved to be too small, but seduced by the Riviera, Elizabeth bought a property with a splendid view near the hilltop village of Mougins – only an olive grove away from H.G. Wells – and named it Le Mas des Roses. On moving in, in September 1930, she decorated the house in pastel shades that matched the flowers in the garden – violet, pink and light green – and lined the terrace with rows of Pallidia irises. Friends brought cuttings, and fifteen months later she wrote in her diary with characteristic wit: 'My garden full of quite unaccountable flowers, such as wallflowers (due in spring), cannas (ought to be over long ago), irises (also due in spring) and masses of stocks. Also the oranges are ripening fast on my two little trees and looking lovely.'

Long associated with Brittany, the already twice-divorced Colette met Maurice Goudeket, a jeweller, who spent his summers near Ste Maxime. By the end of 1925, her first summer there, she had found a little house near the beach in St Tropez: Tamaris-les-Pins which she re-named La Treille Muscate. There were four small rooms and no electricity; a modest dwelling, she admitted, but who would notice amid all the luxuriant foliage? The gate was smothered in oleander and a row of old mimosas led to the front door; there were oranges and figs, a pine wood, a vineyard, and an inexhaustible well. Near the kitchen was a terrace, shaded throughout the day by a huge canopy of wisteria. This became the heart of the household – where she ate, and in the summer dragged her mattress out to sleep.

For Colette, who had been a chatelaine in her previous marriage, it was something of an adventure to furnish the house with just the bare essentials and she derived immense satisfaction from being a gardener, labourer and cook. The house was only a stone's throw from the sea, and every morning she took an early walk, and then, after breakfast, 'sat squarely on the ground and scratched and dug the earth with her

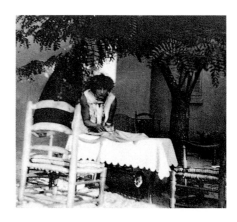

fingers', watched by her French bulldog and black cat. Following the morning's exertions, lunch: crusts of bread soaked in olive oil and rubbed with garlic then sprinkled with *gros sel*. After her siesta, she would sit down to work, turned away from the view in a gloomy corner on an uncomfortable chair. Only the rustling of a page as she threw it off with controlled rage, broke the silence from time to time. Maugham, who thought her 'ease of expression quite formidable' was amazed when she told him she might spend a whole morning on a single page.

At La Treille, Colette wrote *La Naissance du Jour* whose heroine was none other than its author. 'Is this house going to be my last, the one that will find me faithful, the one I shall never leave again? It is so ordinary that it could have no rivals . . . .' Her little garden was equally ordinary: fruit, vegetables and flowers, young tangerine trees, planted – for whom? 'I don't know. Perhaps for me.' At the top of the garden, the sunflowers reigned, each heart was a 'tart of black honeycomb'. The winter brought double narcissi, tiny roses, scented stocks, even lavender. Spring was tender and scented, full of flowering quinces, of lilacs and irises, roses, wisteria and stocks, and of arums 'bigger than the most ancient coronet of sugared almonds.'

It was largely due to Colette's evocative descriptions that *le tout Paris* began to colonize St Tropez. Soon people were coming to stare at her in the garden, or sailing past to watch her swim, while campers pitched their tents on the beach. Eventually it became unbearable, and after thirteen years at La Treille Muscate, where she had been so happy and loved so much, she sold up and left.

The Riviera was a huge melting pot of nationalities and personalities; paths crossed which normally would not have, sometimes with mixed results. Matisse was neither pleased nor flattered to be told by Maugham that his paintings were bought '*pour fleurir ma maison*'. In this salubrious climate gardens figured prominently in the social swim as places where parties were held, and people danced, ate, talked. A mutual interest in gardens also brought people together. The friendship that existed between the Hanburys and Gustave Thuret accounted for many of the plants at La Mortola; while Norah Warre's Garden Book is full of gifts of plants. Dominating Riviera gardening from the 1920s for sixty years were the close friendships between Edith Wharton, Charles de Noailles, Lawrence Johnston, Norah Warre and Basil Leng – the great modern gardeners and plantsmen who pooled their ideas and tastes and shared plants. These were the founder members of what Henriette Chiesa refers to informally as 'the garden club', a close knit group even today.

In the halcyon days of the Riviera, imagination and style flourished against a moneyed background – as personified by Cole and Linda Porter. Although the Porters lived in a Venetian palazzo, they were among the very first to rent Lady Aberconway's Château de la Garoupe – unprecedented in the summer months. Would any garden other than the perfectly situated and

brilliantly landscaped La Garoupe have been able to impress, influence and inspire the American Gerald Murphy – himself a landscape architect turned painter – and his wife Sara to the extent that it spawned Villa America and the earthy yet highly sophisticated cult that grew around it?

The peaceful beauty of La Garoupe's garden enchanted the Murphys, and soon they were looking for one of their own. They found one below Antibes' lighthouse; a house with seven acres of gardens running down towards the 'burnished blue-steel' Mediterranean as Gerald called it. It was an extraordinary garden that had once belonged to a French army officer, a military attache in the Near East. It included pure white Arabian Maples, desert holly and persimmon trees, many varieties of mimosa, eucalyptus, palms, and a genuine cedar of Lebanon. Also pepper trees and olives. Heliotrope ran wild through the garden, which flowed down from the house in a series of levels intersected by gravel paths. There was hardly a flower that would not grow as it was sheltered from the mistral and the scented air was filled with the song of nightingales.

The Murphys renamed the house Villa America. They painted it beige with yellow shutters, and inside the walls were white, the furniture covered in black satin, and the rooms filled with oleanders, tulips, roses, mimosa, heliotrope, jasmine, or camellias picked fresh from the garden every day. They built the first sun roof ever seen on the Riviera, bought rattan café chairs from the dealers who supplied local restaurants, and laid an outdoor terrace of grey and white marble tiles around the silver linden tree under which they dined. Guests at dinner parties on the terrace sat on 'metal chairs painted silver with hot-water radiator finish'.

Although on French soil it remained essentially an American experience – and fascinating to the French. Gerald loved American folk art and collected Negro songs and spirituals which he sang in two part harmony with Sara one evening for Erik Satie. They received all the latest jazz records from America. Their schooner, designed by Diaghilev's cousin, was named *Weatherbird*, after a Louis Armstrong song, and the record was sealed within her keel.

The Murphys were art lovers, and their guests, whatever their nationality, agreed that they were masters of the art of living. Their sunny inventive life attracted like-minded Americans – Dos Passos, Dorothy Parker, Archibald MacLeish – and fascinated F. Scott Fitzgerald, Picasso and Fernand Léger, who drew on elements of the Murphys' style in their work. Gerald was a very good, 'cerebral painter' of the type that inspired pop art, and according to Archibald MacLeish, he and Sara became 'a sort of nexus with everything that was going on'. Though attentive hosts, life revolved around their family, their garden, and the sensuous joy of living on the Riviera. 'The air,' wrote Dos Passos, 'smelt of eucalyptus and tomatoes and heliotrope from the garden.' The Murphy children were fascinated by the long fingernail of Picasso's right pinky that he told them he mixed his paints with. They each had their own vegetable gardens to tend, and pets to look after. Ten-year-old Baoth named one of his chickens Dottie

after Dorothy Parker. It turned out to be a rooster, but nobody minded, least of all Dorothy who was a close friend of theirs. She stayed in the exquisitely decorated guesthouse surrounded by fig trees laden with fruit, which was 'fine' she said with characteristic asperity, 'except that I hate figs in any form'.

At Villa America the Murphy's shared two cows with the Archibald MacLeishes who lived next door, and raised chickens; they made olive oil from their own olives, and harvested and sold the blossoms of the bitter oranges to the perfumeries of Grasse. Their orchards were planted with orange, lemon, tangerine, apricot and nut trees, and Sara's herb garden had over a dozen different varieties. To this quintessentially Riviera garden, she added a patch of American corn and would serve typically American dishes such as poached eggs and Golden Bantam corn cut from the cob and sprinkled with paprika and her homegrown tomatoes cooked in olive oil and garlic.

All the vegetables and fruits came from the garden, and meals were taken under the linden tree on the terrace overlooking the potager beneath. F. Scott Fitzgerald, grown drunk and disorderly one evening, began 'lobbing' tomatoes at the other guests. He was banned from the house for three weeks, principally because of the distress caused to the old gardener, Joseph. What's more, noted Dos Passos, the tomatoes had been particularly fine that year. Unperturbed, Fitzgerald modelled Rosemary and Dick Diver in *Tender is the Night*, on the Murphys. 'The golden couple that he and Zelda dreamed of becoming actually existed,

VIBRANT BOUGAINVILLAEA CLOTHES THE FACADE OF CHATEAU DE LA GAROUPE THAT SO ENCHANTED COLE PORTER, F. SCOTT FITZGERALD AND GERALD AND SARA MURPHY.

17

THE 1910 VENETIAN PALAZZINO OF VILLA ROTHSCHILD – ITS GARDEN WAS THE ULTIMATE IN MANICURED FRENCH EXOTIC STYLE. THOUSANDS OF TONS OF EARTH WERE BROUGHT IN TO BUILD IT.

Fortunatus incarnate,' commented Dos Passos. Having rented a villa nearby, Fitzgerald came every day and followed them around for weeks, asking questions in an intrusive and irritating manner about every aspect of their life. Sara didn't like the novel. She found it shallow, and wrote 'I can't help wishing we were in some other book.'

The Murphys first four years at Villa America had been golden years. But then the golden bowl broke. In October 1929, their nine-year-old son Patrick contracted tuberculosis, and Gerald put away his brushes forever. They fought his illness for seven years but lost the battle. In the meantime, Baoth, their elder son, died of spinal meningitis. 'For me, only the invented part of our life had any scheme, any real meaning, or beauty,' wrote Gerald. 'Life itself has stepped in now, and scarred and blundered and destroyed.'

The gardens thus worked on several levels – as influences, social venues, and places to live in; each with its own style. The English excelled at plantsman's gardens, the French produced botanical triumphs or gardens which showed a completely original vision like those of Ferdinand Bac, Coco Chanel and now Nicole de Vésian. Gardens were also made that indulged the whims of the very wealthy; still with us today is that of the eccentric Victorian collector Baroness Ephrussi de Rothschild. Her much visited pink palazzo was built purely to display the galaxy of art treasures she had acquired from all over the world, while the main purpose of the garden was to house her stone artefacts.

ABOVE: VENETIAN
COLONNADES, TUSCAN
CYPRESSES AND MODERN
POTTERY ASSEMBLED HERE AS
YOU WOULD NEVER SEE THEM
IN AN ITALIAN GARDEN.

Landscaped in the characteristic formal French exotic style, it embodied everything the purists railed against.

There were gardens of ideas like Fontana Rosa, Blasco Ibañez's extraordinary Novelist's Garden – all dappled light, fragrance, fish shimmering in fountains and pools, pillars and benches decorated by vivid turquoise, rose and yellow ceramic tiles.

By the time the flamboyant Vicente Blasco Ibañez settled in Menton in 1922, aged fifty-five, he had led an Homeric existence as a globe-trotting political revolutionary and novelist. Opposed to monarchy and dictatorship, anti-conformist and anti-clerical he had studied law and then founded Spain's first socialist newspaper. After fighting many political duels, attempting to start a revolution, and being jailed thirty times for his trouble, he finally fled Spain.

Missing a genial climate, Ibañez had come to the Riviera in 1916 in search of a home, and finally settled on Fontana Rosa, a Belle Epoque villa, sumptuously clad in exotica – ficus, banana, eucalyptus, and palms – at the bottom of a steeply descending hillside of narrow terraces planted with agrumes and olives. He arrived with his wife, a chauffeur and butler, his wife's *dame de companie*, a secretary, cook, servants, and four gardeners – and for the next seven years until his death established a final colony within his own garden walls. We owe this garden to Ibañez' painful exile. Passionately committed to

BELOW: VICENTE BLASCO
IBANEZ SEEN WITH HIS SON
SIGFRIDO AND WIFE ELENA ON
ONE OF THE CERAMIC
BENCHES AT FONTANA ROSA.

a country that had rejected him and to which he would now never return, he sought in his advancing years to recreate the home lost to him.

Hollywood bought the film rights to several of his novels, notably *The Four Horsemen of the Apocalypse*, which launched the career of Rudolph Valentino, so Ibañez was able to spend prodigiously on Fontana Rosa. He parted with 3,000,000 francs in gold, and oversaw all the work personally. A summer residence was built in the lower part of the garden to keep cool, and at the top he added one for the winter months. He constructed a library to house his twenty thousand books, a cinema, and apartments for guests, who included Greta Garbo, Valentino and Rex Ingram when they were in Nice filming *Mare Nostrum*, Ibañez' anti-war novel. Outside, on pedestals he placed all over the garden, were the busts of his literary idols – from Dostoevsky and Dickens to Victor Hugo.

Born into a working class family, the young Vicente had played in the public gardens of Valencia as a child; little gardens of high walls and columns, fountains and pergolas, and benches decorated with colourful ceramics with a Moorish influence. Ibañez imported these from Manises, a small town near Valencia; certainly Fontana Rosa's relief tiles came from here as well as the majority of blue and red examples. Others, the orange and lemon ones, were made locally in the town of Menton.

He brought the very earth of Valencia by the sackful. In it he grew pomegranates and jasmines, lilies, oranges and the rose and carnation cuttings which he had sent over from the gardens he knew as a child. Cinerarias, santolina and veronica grew in clumps beneath the palms; camellias and fuchsia behind the benches. It was a tranquil, fragrant garden, with dappled shade under rose-laden pergolas, beneath plane trees and magnolias. As in many Riviera gardens, exotic pets had their place too. An aquarium embellished with Ionian and Doric columns housed fish, which he exchanged with the newly built Museum of

Oceanography in Monte Carlo. They swam in the *bassins* and even in the fountains. Birds sang in the aviary, and the garden was freshened by the play of water. It was atmospheric and artfully orchestrated.

'When I am tired of working,' he wrote, 'I go out to the lower garden, I climb the stairs to the upper garden and contemplate the immensity of the Mediterranean, the bays and the promontories of the Alpes Maritimes, and I return to my library to write. My garden is a work tool, maybe the most important of all.' Thus restored, he could continue the enormous output of work without, he said, damaging his health. He died nevertheless at the age of sixty-one. After Franco's death, Spain decided it was safe to bring Ibañez home. Freddie Braun can remember the Spanish naval warships in the harbour; the guns, the fanfare, the salutes as the coffin was carried on board. He was buried in his beloved Valencia, home at last. His home on the Riviera, however, has been treated less kindly.

Ibañez had wanted his garden to offer solace to ageing writers, as it had done for him. His son Sigfrido

THE NEWLY RESTORED HEMICYCLE AT FONTANA ROSA THAT IBANEZ DEDICATED TO CERVANTES. IT DEPICTS A HUNDRED SCENES FROM HIS NOVEL DON QUIXOTE.

sold the top half of the garden to developers in 1970, and gave the bottom half to the city. Twenty years later it was classed as a *Monument Historique*. By that time Fontana Rosa lay in ruins, the house had been demolished, and there was only enough money to restore the Cervantes hemicycle. The town of Menton has suggested that the library could be restored, integrated with the garden and opened to the public. Funds could be raised for its upkeep by selling copies of the tiles. But the city of Valencia has not contributed a single peseta. Perhaps they will wait until the garden, too, is dead.

Scarcely less flamboyant and visually startling than the garden of Blasco Ibañez was the whole aura surrounding Roderick ('Rory') Cameron, travel writer, 'garden decorator', and his mother, the 'much married and very beautiful' Countess of Kenmare, who lived like gods in a Palladian villa on Cap Ferrat. Their house was adorned by vast arrangements of sunflowers on Louis XV tables, and tubs of bursting peonies, while outside the trunks and lower branches of the orange trees were bared and painted with lime wash solely to produce a glowing theatrical effect. There is a memorable description of mother and son greeting their guests on the marble steps of La Fiorentina: Rory, 'six-feet tall with sapphire eyes', the much married and very beautiful Countess, dressed 'in a striking gold shot sari, roped in pearls, a scarlet parrot perched on one of her shoulders and on a double leash a pair of baby cheetahs'.

A HEDGE OF CYPRESSES FOLLOWS THE LINE OF CITRUS TREES AND PILLARS. THE FRUIT HANGING ON THE TREES ARE REPEATED THROUGHOUT THE GARDEN AS MOTIFS ON CERAMIC TILES.

21

Exotic pets and birds, perhaps the ultimate garden accessory, were a regular feature. The tradition originated in Italy and first appeared in the fifteenth-century garden of the good King René in Aix as a zoological menagerie, including camels, dromedaries, elephants, bears and often ostriches. Sometimes these garden ornaments seem to have got rather out of hand: the English actress Maxine Elliott shared her house with 'monkeys and half mad wild deer', while the white peacocks of the American sculptor Henry Clews at La Napoule regularly brought the *Train Bleu* to a standstill. Brightly plumed exotic birds calling and squawking through the trees undoubtedly added to the already tropical and socially rarified ambience.

The shrill calls of these bright birds through the gardens contrasted with the 'big silent cars' that rolled up the drives and came to symbolize this era: the chauffeured Rolls-Royces and Bentleys that purred smoothly between luncheons, teas and dinners in each other's houses. Consuelo Vanderbilt Balsan, the former Duchess of Marlborough, whose luncheons sometimes included eleven different nationalities, describes all her guests setting off after lunch in their Rolls and Bentleys, evoking a bizarre image of a 'cavalcade of cars with spades and trowels to dig up the wild flowers of the Alps, to transplant them to our gardens'. Maugham and Lord Beaverbrook exchanged avocados and figs from their respective gardens by means of their respective chauffeured Rolls-Royces. Edith Wharton used to be driven in hers to the heights of Hyères, so that she might take her daily constitutional and walk down again; or to her innumerable picnics which Kenneth Clark said were preceded with endless fuss and always went badly. Coco Chanel and Colette took off in Chanel's chauffeured Rolls over the *arrière pays* in search of craftsmen. A Bentley for Lawrence Johnston's mother, a sporty Lancia for him, and when he set off on his plant-hunting safaris it was not a hike with a knapsack and vasculum, but a luxurious expedition that included his Italian valet-cook and chauffeur.

The infrastructure that permitted this very pleasant life – and in the absence of which gardens now look completely different – was the army of gardeners and servants. The employers depended on their staff to open and close their houses, and were waited on hand and foot. On one occasion, Edith Wharton went to live in a hotel because her staff were indisposed, and another year attributed the lack of any flowers in her garden to having had to dismiss her gardener for dishonesty. The reason for Coco Chanel's buffet lunches, attended by Winston Churchill, being considered such a racy novelty – almost a caprice – was that the servants had been dismissed for the afternoon! A visitor to Alice de Rothschild's garden at Villa Victoria once quipped that every twenty metres a gardener stood waiting for a leaf to fall so that he might pick it up – which may not be far from the truth, as she employed fifty full-time gardeners who were seasonally supplemented with thirty or forty more. They wore the blue and yellow of the Rothschild colours, their rank in the hierarchy revealed by the colour of their hats. Without them, these gardens wouldn't have existed at all, though so highhanded were the likes of Maybud Campbell and

MARCEL GAUCHER, THE HEAD GARDENER'S SON, IN VILLA VICTORIA. ALTHOUGH THE GARDEN WAS NAMED AFTER THE QUEEN, ALICE DE ROTHSCHILD HAD NO QUALMS ABOUT ORDERING HER OFF THE LAND AND WAS SUBSEQUENTLY REFERRED TO BY THE MONARCH AS THE 'ALL POWERFUL ONE'.

Alice de Rothschild that one wonders why their staff stayed.

There were resounding battles conducted between the head gardeners who had been trained in Italy and indoctrinated by the rigid and regimental way of gardening, and the English owners who, for example, didn't like pruning their olives. One gardener who arrived in an English garden as a boy of fourteen with no training, and therefore no prejudices, and who stayed on for sixty years was Mario Lavagna, whose warm relationship with all three generations of Waterfields at the Clos du Peyronnet is commemorated by a plaque. Humphrey Waterfield used to say that if you have a gardener long enough, the garden becomes his. Colette's gardener was not impressed with her carefree, anarchic garden and promised to make her a true Provençal garden. The result, she said, looked like a barbeque grill.

Left to their own devices within the confines of these grand gardens in the company of gardeners and governesses, were children like the young Kenneth Clark and Michael J. Arlen, their sensibility nurtured by childhood winters spent on the Riviera. The Clarks lived initially on their yacht and then in a villa constructed so solidly by the Scottish builders, that the subsequent owner found it impossible to demolish. It had been an extravagance for the short time spent there, but 'my father had his gambling and my mother had her garden'. An isolated, yet self-contained child, Kenneth was content to play in the garden with his blue frog Jaqueline and a parrot his father had bought in Monte Carlo that perched on his shoulder squawking 'mind your own bloody

THE FRONT ELEVATION OF THE LATE-19TH CENTURY VILLA, CLOS DU PEYRONNET. THE ITALIAN BORDER IS ON THE MOUNTAIN THAT MAKES A STARK BACKGROUND TO THE GARDEN'S RICHNESS. THE ANDUZE JARS BEHIND THE TALL PALM, BRAHEA ARMATA, ARE FROM SERRE DE LA MADONE. ON THE FACADE ARE TREE PEONIES, AND A COLUMN COLLAPSING IN THE TIGHT CLUTCH OF WISTERIA.

business' to all who passed. He also had a friend in the ancient Empress Eugénie. He recalls walking with her in the olive groves – a lyrical image dispelled by the young Jean Cocteau who also walked with this ancient Empress and remembers something quite different. 'The Empress detested flowers: she cudgelled them with her straight handled cane, beat them out of her path. So it was a dry garden we walked through, all rocks and cactus, a true Spanish garden whose stiff plants bristled with all the daggers of the Madonna.'

Michael J. Arlen (son of the Michael Arlen who had established himself with his Riviera novel *The Green Hat*), remembered visits to his great-grandmother Madame La Princesse Daria Kara-Georgevitches, who lived in the huge Villa Fiorentina in Cannes 'with its endless terraces of Italianate gardens (box hedges garishly trimmed into shapes of animals, birds and whatnot), footmen, camellias . . . I used to go there sometimes for lunch. The two of us (only one footman). Lamb chops. Mint sauce. The smell of mint everywhere. Sunlight. She had very white hair then, and a kind, no nonsense smile. I don't remember what we talked about. And afterwards we'd sit for a while outside, and we would read, and fall asleep, and I'd throw gravel at the peacocks.' Arlen sensed that moment at the end of the 1930s when the long shadow of war began to chill the air and harden the warm golden light. 'All those bright, bright whites and blues beside the Mediterranean. And then it had all begun to go. The sun on the white houses. The sun on the Mediterranean. The sun on everything. Even as a kid I can remember it changing . . . . My father listening each evening to the BBC's Empire Service. Fouchard, the old gardener absently oiling his 1918 rifle.'

The children who grew up in gardens made special by their parents, never found that magic anywhere else. Somerset Maugham commented, 'An unhappy childhood is the making of you otherwise you have already had the best'. Maugham's *Of Human Bondage* based on his own childhood remained the best book he ever wrote.

Those great days on the Riviera when people could devote themselves entirely to their gardens are long since gone. The gardens designed by Harold Peto have disappeared; his Villa Rosmarino is still standing, but in ruins, inhabited by squatters. Well over fifty years have passed since the heyday, and many gardens, stylish and simple, have disappeared with their gardeners. They are memorable now for the happiness they brought, the friendships they initiated, and also for the plants culled from every corner of the earth. Coaxed into flourishing often thousands of miles from home in this enormous experimental outdoor greenhouse by the sea, they still enhance many a garden.

What happened between the time these English garden makers first pitched their tents a hundred and fifty years ago on this small strip of rocky coastline surrounded by mountains is unique and will never be seen again. It was invented, reinvented and finally ruined by foreigners: tourism, that greatest of modern carbuncles, eventually claims every unspoiled spot everywhere, so that now only inhospitable frontiers are left. Paradises like the virginal Riviera have been ruined the world over, but it is tourism, ironically, that now funds the botanical gardens, in the way that big corporations sponsor most of the arts.

Lawrence Johnston's Hidcote garden was the first property to be taken on by the National Trust on the merit of its garden alone. Its

THE LIME TREES ARE CLIPPED TO ECHO THE HORSE-SHOE CURVE IN BOX. THE 12TH CENTURY CHATEAU DE GOURDON WAS RESTORED IN 1919 BY AN AMERICAN, MISS NORRIS, AND CONVERTED INTO A MUSEUM TO HOUSE HER COLLECTION OF PRIMITIVE ART.

French counterpart, Serre de la Madone, having been stripped of all its rarer specimens soon after Johnston's death, but otherwise untouched, has gone quietly to sleep. This is perhaps preferable to the municipal nightmare that has been dreamt up for Edith Wharton's garden in Hyères. The French and, in view of the huge battle to save La Mortola, the Italians give priority to safeguarding their bricks and mortar: a garden is not regarded as a valuable part of the national heritage. French enthusiasm for plants has always been directed at the botanists, whose approach was scientific and concentrated on collections.

The gardens that have remained impervious to changing garden fashion and to foreigners, have been the 'green gardens'. The *grands seigneurs* who made the great box parterres like Ansouis and Beauregard and the hanging gardens of Gourdon consigned their heirs to a lifetime of clipping, as curators to museum pieces. Every September the Duc de Clarens gets out his shears and clips the parterre at Beauregard as generations have done before him. It has grown a good deal higher and wider, of course, but still retains the shape of the Maltese Cross. The setting is so isolated that fifteen servants came and went in three months and only his Irish wife felt at home there. Another garden to emerge unscathed from the ravages of the century is that of Orves, in Hyères, which belongs to painter Pierre Deval. His daughter Françoise is now busily filling the parterres with a great diversity of plants, an enthusiasm that grew during her many years spent in England.

THE PARTERRE OF CHATEAU DE BEAUREGARD WAS ORIGINALLY DESIGNED AS A MALTESE CROSS.

It is the chronic lament of everyone who knew the Riviera as it once was that the best is gone, and this sense of a lost paradise is part of the poignancy of the story. Yet the vines and the cypresses, the fragrant mimosa and eucalyptus, the 'musical comedy palms' all settled in at last, have made the Riviera their home, and the air still retains that intoxicating luminosity, in the presence of which everything else can somehow be forgiven. In selected nooks and crannies, behind tall hedges, high up in the hills, the frontiers stretching to Provence, the quixotic adventure of garden-making continues here undaunted. Thus the story of gardeners and their gardens on the Riviera does not end – for those who persevere, and who adapt, the love affair remains fresh and exciting. And as Michael J. Arlen concluded comfortingly, 'the Mediterranean is still the Mediterranean.'

THE PAINTER PIERRE DEVAL AT ORVES, A GARDEN HE HAS NURTURED FOR NEARLY SEVENTY-FIVE YEARS.

Chapter One
ENGLISH GARDENS AND GARDENERS

•

I can scarcely help thinking myself enchanted. The small extent of country which I see is all cultivated like a garden. Indeed the plain presents nothing but gardens full of green trees, loaded with oranges, lemons, citrons and bergamots which make a delightful appearance . . . roses, carnations, ranunculas, anemonies and daffodils, blowing in full glory with such beauty, vigour, and perfume, as no flower in England ever exhibited.

TOBIAS SMOLLETT, NICE, 1765

T HE ENGLISH COLONIZATION OF THE RIVIERA BEGAN WITH three intrepid travellers: Dr Tobias Smollett, Dr James Henry Bennet and Lord Brougham, who hoisted the Union Jack over their newly 'discovered' territories – Nice, Menton and Cannes respectively. Dr Smollett, who described the countryside as an enchanted garden, was reputedly the first person to bathe in the sea; Dr Bennet, who promoted Menton as a winter haven for consumptives, soon started experimenting with exotic and native plants alike. He opened his garden to the public every morning – a public which included Queen Victoria. Lord Brougham, on his way to the Savoie with his ailing daughter in 1834, was diverted to Cannes because of a cholera epidemic. He fell in love with the small fishing village and within a week was strutting around his own piece of land, planning a villa and urging well-connected friends to do likewise. His villa was christened Château Eléonore, after his daughter, who died in 1839. 'I dip my feet into the Mediterranean,' he said – the orange groves, almond trees and vineyards 'reaching to its edge'. The serenity was belied by a shocking description of the great Lord Chancellor by that other eminent English chronicler of the Riviera, Augustus Hare, who saw Brougham frequently. 'He was the most disagreeable, selfish, cantankerous, violent old man who ever lived. He used to swear by the hour together at his sister-in-law, Mrs William Brougham, who ever lived with him, and bore his ill-treatment with consummate patience . . . Though a proper carriage was always provided for him, he would insist upon driving

THE 'IMBRICATION' OF FOLIAGE OF TETRAPANAX FRAMES AND ECHOS THE SPIKEY JAGGED SHAPES OF ALOES, AGAVES AND PALM. THIS TETRAPANAX WAS PLANTED BY THE SCHNEIDER SISTERS AFTER NORAH WARRE'S DEATH, IN AN EXAMPLE OF IMAGINATIVE RESTORATION THAT REMAINS FAITHFUL TO THE SPIRIT OF THE GARDEN.

about Cannes daily in the most disreputable old fly he could procure, with the hope that people would say he was neglected by his family.' Should a guest aggravate him during dinner, it was said, he would throw his napkin in the offender's face. Brougham had, however, a particular prestige in Cannes through having made it fashionable. Mrs William Brougham was the wife of the second Lord Brougham who, before his death, had the gardens at the Villa Eléonore redesigned in 1865 by his brother-in-law the great French botanist, nurseryman and rose specialist Gilbert Nabonnand and there bred, from *Rosa gigantea*, 'La Folette' and 'General Schablikine'.

The first Lord Brougham had dubbed England 'Fogland', and his lyrical evocations of Cannes soon caught the imagination of other rich foglanders; by 1879 there were already fifty hotels, many spacious villas and some early estate agents. In search of their ever-flowering, evergreen paradise which knew no winter, they sought to make the ideal *English* garden. Deciduous trees replaced evergreens, cypresses were used in rows as windbreaks, and there were some curious excesses: notably a garden shaped like a boat, and another filled with three hundred and fifty thousand potted plants. None of the locals could understand this obsession with green lawns which required constant watering and served no useful purpose. Amongst the fiercest critics was the Englishman, Augustus Hare.

> *The hills are covered with hideous villas, chiefly built by rich Englishmen, whose main object seems to be the effacement of all the natural beauties of the place – to sow grass which will never live, to import from the north shrubs which cannot grow, and to cut down and root up all the original woods and flowers.*

Undeterred, the foglanders even brought their own turf from England, making croquet lawns bordered by silver ewers in which the players could rinse their hands. When they became bored with croquet, the turf was adapted for lawn tennis. Alice de Rothschild's gardeners poured two tons of grass seed per year on to acres and acres of laboriously raked compost, which was then covered with peat. Somerset Maugham was *still* digging and replanting his grass in 1965.

Baronne Alice de Rothschild really belongs in a chapter named 'The Tale of Three Imperious Spinsters', which Beatrix Potter would have been amused to write, fond as she was of satire. Ellen Willmott and

MAYBUD CAMPBELL PICKING CAMELLIAS AT VAL RAHMEH.

Maybud Campbell would have completed the trio of martinets – all very capable and knowledgeable plantswomen, but remembered chiefly for their intransigent personalities.

Alice de Rothschild had been the chatelaine of Waddesdon Manor, in 'Rothschildshire', for her bachelor brother Ferdinand, and had started overwintering on the Riviera in 1887. A 'plain and solitary girl', she had compensated for an inability to socialize by becoming a gardener, and deployed her talents first at Eythorpe and then at Waddesdon. She found the coast vulgar, so at the age of forty-one began to build herself a house in Grasse, going on to make perhaps the most ostentatious garden ever seen.

A FIELD OF LAVENDER ABOVE
BONNIEUX, NEAR NICOLE DE
VESIAN'S HOUSE.

The surrounding landscape was a chequerboard pattern of fields of flowers grown for the perfumeries of Grasse – jasmine, May roses, tuberoses, lavender, orange blossom and scented geraniums. Alice bought a hundred hectares of terraced hillside and immediately proceeded to landscape the ancient terraces into rolling parkland, where she planted citrus trees by the hundred, arranged in groups to make them appear more natural and 'integrate' with the landscape.

Hers was the ultimate 'exotic' garden for Augustus Hare, Maupassant and Mérimée to complain about. It contained an enormous collection of ornamental plants: palms twenty metres high, *Yucca folifera* ten metres high, bamboos with thick trunks, a 'debauchery' of agaves and flaming aloes.

Along the public highway that bisects the estate, mimosas of every species had been grafted on to small trees for a shrubby effect, and flowering was continuous from November to May. After negotiations with the local 'highways department', her gardeners tended both the mimosas and the road, brushing off the dust – and equine offerings.

The garden had everything, and in great quantities; a reconstituted *paysage provençal*, with 1,446 olive trees, underplanted with as many

FIELDS OF POPPIES ON THE
WAY FROM THE COAST TO THE
JARDIN ALPIN DU LAUTARET.

beds of both Parma and common violets, raised by a specialist from Hyères. Alice advised her gardeners to plant yellow and white between clashing colours – a spectacle that would make even a municipal gardener blush, but with bedding and borders overflowing with fifty-five thousand daisies, twenty-five thousand stocks and five thousand myosotis, perhaps no one would notice! There was a rock garden, a winter flowering grotto, and a spectacular three-kilometre drive designed with hairpin bends; around every corner lay a surprise, the planting becoming progressively wilder and the panorama extending itself further and further, the higher one climbed. At the entrance were a few dozen specimens of palms, agaves and aloes, then a thirty-metre retaining rockery wall planted with perennials; around the next bend, lawns carpeted with spring bulbs, followed by a wood underplanted with lavender, rosemary and citronella; higher still, a cascade and miniature lake with a wild-looking rockery beneath; and finally, at the very top – what else but a Tea Pavilion.

Alice de Rothschild laid out all these gardens herself, without the help of a landscape architect; instead, she would invite knowledgeable and useful people to lunch, and pick their brains. They, of course, were only too happy to oblige. She went to the best nurseries and not only chose the plants herself but supervised their planting.

During the blazing heat of summer, the estate being surrounded by pine forests, gardeners would be posted every Sunday to the tops of the hills to watch for fires. October brought the grand arrival: her chauffeured Rolls-Royce, having preceded her from England, would collect her from the station in Cannes. At the villa, the red carpet was rolled out and the staff lined up to greet her. The mayor always sent a representative, which irritated her intensely. After a rest, she would inspect the garden and fresh green lawns with the head gardener, Monsieur Gaucher, who was required to wear a bowler hat at all times. His son, Marcel, was born on the estate and, even after Alice's death in 1922, continued to work for the Rothschild family for the rest of his life. He recalled in his memoirs that Alice never once spoke to him. To the child she was but a starched silhouette, *'la tenue vestimentaire immuable'*; with a grey floor-length skirt, her face hidden under a mauve veil and straw hat almost like a bee-keeper's, and holding a silver hoe with an ebony handle – ready to slay the first weed.

Alice de Rothschild was extravagant and capricious, and could afford to be; while no less extravagant and capricious, Maybud Campbell could not. Daughter of a wealthy Scottish doctor, she was a botanist and singer who lived at Val Rahmeh, Menton. For twenty years she exasperated friends and staff alike: her head gardener and maid, Raymond and Marguerite Arsento, struggled with her fickle temperament yet remained magnetized by her aristocratic bearing.

Like so many Victorian spinsters, she lived with her parents until they died, and did not buy her own home, Val Rahmeh, until she was in her mid-fifties. Originally a farm, it had been acquired in 1905 by Lord Radcliffe, the former governor of Malta, who had built a Mediterranean-style villa and planted citrus trees. Rahmeh in Hindi means cats – Lord Radcliffe's passion, and one shared by Maybud Campbell. She had fourteen of them, and ran the household according to her favourite cat Charley's whims.

Monsieur and Madame Arsento have a son, Hubert, who is the present head gardener and now regards the garden as his own. The world of Miss Campbell was his youth; a childhood spent in the presence of English nobility, *une grande dame*. 'She accepted that I was there, but it was also understood that I didn't make any noise. There were times when I saw her walking about in her garden like a little girl. She was very rude and authoritative with the servants, but once she'd crossed the threshold into the garden she was a child. In the evenings she took a basket and we cut flowers together. Then Miss Campbell went into the hall to arrange the bouquets into marvellous confections of flowers and green branches. She had stayed a child – made capricious because she never grew up. Sometimes she'd sing; not often, but when she arranged the bouquets her voice filled the house. Then suddenly the mood changed. Miss Campbell was a very beautiful woman, and when she was nice you would have given her anything; when she had money she was very generous. But who could put up with her? Nobody.' Her staff, three maids and a cook, dressed in black with starched white aprons, stood rigidly to attention when she passed, as though she was the Queen of England herself.

Like her father, Maybud Campbell was an amateur botanist and collected seeds and cuttings on her trips to Italy. She was also considered the local expert on myrtles, and had a fine collection of crinums. Reckless extravagance and a feckless lover swiftly pared her fortune and her debts mounted. In 1966, although she'd been offered two million francs

CLIMBERS SWATHE THE FRONT COURTYARD AT VAL RAHMEH: FROM LEFT TO RIGHT DATURA ARBOREA, BEAUMONTIA GRANDIFLORA, AND THE RED HOLMSKIOLDIA SANGUINEA; BETWEEN THE BENCHES HIBISCUS, AND ON THE RIGHT, THOUGH NOT IN FLOWER, SOLANUM WENDLANDII. CREEPING ALONG THE TERRACE IS CARISSA SPINARUM.

by developers who wanted to raze it and put up apartments, Val Rahmeh was sold to the Musée de l'Homme for one million francs in order to preserve the garden. Under the direction of Professor Yves Monnier, the museum's agenda is to turn Val Rahmeh into a real botanical garden which will earn its keep and survive. He and Hubert Arsento are planning to extend their collection of Chinese plants, subtropical plants, and rare ornamentals in an effort to offer something different to the other gardens. At the same time, Monnier wants to respect the form and the structure of the garden as laid out and planted by Miss Campbell.

Maybud Campbell died alone eleven years later in a small flat in Roquebrune, with the blazing heat of summer and the cold light of impecunity staring her in the face. The imperious voice, the pervasive scent exist only in the memories of Raymond and Marguerite, now the caretakers, and their son Hubert. To them the garden is not merely a collection of interesting trees and plants inspected daily by the general public, but of plants that are part of Miss Campbell's life, and they are sincerely grieved when something she had planted dies. Their recollections reawaken the garden once more, evoking an era we shall never see again. When their chapter closes, so will hers.

The Famous Five: Thomas and Daniel Hanbury, Ellen Willmott, Lady Aberconway, the Waterfields and Norah Warre came specifically to the Riviera to make gardens, each with something different in mind. Botanical pursuits governed the Hanbury and Willmott gardens; Lady Aberconway and Humphrey Waterfield were driven by a genuine love of visual beauty; while Norah Warre and, now, Humphrey Waterfield's nephew William continue the tradition of English plantmanship that began over a hundred and fifty years ago in a Clapham pharmacy.

SIR THOMAS HANBURY IS ON THE LEFT OF THIS FAMILY GROUP AT LA MORTOLA.

La Mortola

THE HANBURYS

La Mortola is in every sense the English flagship of the Riviera. It has stayed the longest and most complex course of any of the gardens; battered by two World Wars, neglected, and periodically ravaged by a capricious climate. During the last thirty years, it has been passed like the proverbial parcel from one Italian quango to the other – except that, in this version, the music never stops.

Born into the financial security provided by the pharmaceutical firm Allen and Hanbury, Thomas Hanbury nevertheless set off at the age of eighteen to make his own fortune in Shanghai, which in 1853 had only been an 'open' port for ten years. Although the city was under seige by rebels, he established himself as a respected and successful silk and tea merchant. Meanwhile his elder brother Daniel, a pharmaceutical chemist, stayed in London to pursue his own studies into the specific botanical origins of the many drugs inaccurately identified on London's

OPPOSITE: GERANIUM PALMATUM, A BIENNIAL PLANT FROM THE CANARY ISLANDS, IS GROWN AS GROUND COVER AT THE BOTTOM OF THE GARDEN.

THIS GROTTO IS NAMED THE FONTANA DEL DRAGO AND THE BRONZE FIGURE CAME FROM KYOTO. EGYPTIAN PAPYRUS AND THE PAPER REED FLOURISH HERE FED BY MOUNTAIN SPRINGS.

drug and spice markets. Daniel's colleague Professor Fluckiger described him as 'truth, every inch of him'. A scientist and a scholar, he was a frugal man, arriving at the office from his Clapham home with a green baize bag containing specimens of materia medica, letters and his lunch, which consisted of an apple or an orange and a Bath Oliver biscuit. He went on a plant-hunting expedition to the Holy Land with Joseph Hooker, Director of Kew Gardens where he gathered samples for his own collection. For his work on Indian and Chinese materia medica he obtained many specimens by correspondence and others were sent by his brother Thomas. These he could observe growing in his greenhouses in Clapham. He often had to learn languages and dialects to be able to decipher local papers written about his plants' culture and origin.

In 1864, while trying to identify the adulterant of what was being passed off as Otto of Roses, Daniel took a 'chemist's holiday' to the Riviera. As he was painting, walking and botanizing his way along the coast, he came upon a promontory close to Menton called Punta della Mortola, where on the site of an old fort a lonely ruined palazzo stood surrounded by olive terraces. He was impressed enough to describe it to his brother as the possible site for a botanical garden. Three years were to pass before Thomas, also holidaying in Menton, saw it for himself, this time from the sea. He was wealthy enough, at the age of thirty-five, to be able to 'retire' and pursue his own interests, and although he and Daniel had lived half a world apart for twenty years, they still shared a love of travel, of sunshine and of plants. Here lay the opportunity to indulge in all three. Thomas wanted it recorded, however, that the initiative for the garden came from Daniel.

Beneath the leaking roof of the ruined palazzo Orengo lived a curious group: an old peasant and his wife, their goats and mules, who had munched their way through every edible shade of green vegetation on the promontory, and swallows and bats. Also floating around apparently was the ghost of the nun, Violante, who had sold the original fort to the Marchese Orengo in 1620. She was still reported to be out and about four hundred years later by Sir Thomas's daughter-in-law, Dorothy Hanbury!

The prospect of a haunted palazzo on a small plot of land consisting of limestone and rock – poor soil in which only a few cypresses had managed to survive – and without the guarantee of any more land being available, did not seem to bother Thomas. By May the purchase had been completed and the promontory was his. Work started immediately, and for several months Thomas lived in the village – preferable perhaps to the company of a spectral nun. Daniel arrived in July; his first task being to restore the natural vegetation with seeds of holm oaks, Aleppo pines, holly, *Rhamnus alaternus*, cistus, citrus and coronilla. At the same time he introduced fennel and *Erigeron mucronatus* to the garden which subsequently naturalized along the coast. To obtain his plants he wrote begging letters to friends and contacts. 'I am ambitious,' he wrote to a friend in the Cape, 'to see it stocked with all the rare and precious shrubs that can be grown in that spot without much attention and gardening skill. Our grounds are close to the shore but slope backwards by terraces to five hundred feet above the sea level. There is a tenacious loamy soil, and vegetable mould and sand are not procurable in plenty. The summer drought is considerable and paucity of water is a frequent source of anxiety.'

LA MORTOLA PHOTOGRAPHED AROUND 1870 MUCH AS IT LOOKED WHEN DANIEL HANBURY FIRST SAW IT.

For a year the two bachelor brothers were their own gardeners, returning each autumn to plant passion flowers, peonies and a cedar of Lebanon. From their father's garden in Clapham they brought three dozen different rose varieties; and soon others began arriving from rather more esoteric sources: *Rosa × fortuneana*, found by Mr Fortune in the garden of a rich mandarin in Nighpo; *Rosa damascena* and *Rosa trigintipetala*, presents from King Ferdinand of Bulgaria from the rose fields of Kazanlik near the Shipka Pass, and many others.

A LITTLE LIGHT GARDENING.

As the momentum of the garden grew, and they sought to acclimatize plants culled, cajoled and received as gifts from all corners of the globe, the collections of plants became more and more exotic. Over the years both brothers had courted medical men and consuls, missionaries and curators of museums, conservators of forests and overseers of factories. All these associates were called upon to provide information or specimens. From Southern Arabia came acanthus (now naturalized like a weed along the coast);

from the Jardin d'Essai in Algeria, bamboos and bougainvillaeas; from Abyssinia, juniperus; and from the curiously named southern African country of Pondoland, *Podranea*.

Daniel was particularly interested in obtaining plants that could be of pharmaceutical or economic importance. He therefore tried those that were useful in other countries, such as the Argan tree of Morocco from which an oil is made, and the 'naras' of south-west Africa, chief food of the Hottentots (failed to survive the winter); *Agave weberi*, from which the Mexican drink pulque is made; *Aloe ferox*, the medicinal aloe of Natal; *Catha edulis*, known as 'Kat' in Southern Arabia, whose leaves the Arabs use both for a stimulant and for tea; *Urginea maritima*, an efficacious rat poison, and *Umbellularia californica*, which causes violent sneezing – useful perhaps to rid oneself of tiresome guests.

E.H. Wilson brought them *Clematis armandii* and *meyeniana* from his expeditions to China; Mr Wilson Saunders of Reigate gave them sixty-six species of agave; from Veitch and Sons came the first *Agapanthus umbellatus*, planted in 1868. A great many iris and pelargoniums came from Miss Ellen Willmott, and many species, including *Dianthus arboreus*, from Kew.

Local nurserymen included Gustave Thuret in Antibes and Charles Huber at Hyères, who supplied acacias and Australian species; and from the great botanist Gilbert Nabonnand, of Golfe Juan, they received fifty varieties of acacia, twenty of callistemon, cistus, forty species of eucalyptus, ficus, genista, magnolias, melaleucas, juniperus, yuccas and wigandia. Their citrus collection rapidly grew in size and stature to include the bergamot from Montpelier and *Citrus medica*, known as 'Buddha's Fingers', introduced in 1869 from Thomas's garden in Shanghai. La Mortola was becoming a true botanical garden, and priority was given to acclimatizing and cultivating the new acquisitions. They were planted in a suitable spot as they arrived, but whether or not it was aesthetically pleasing neither brother cared. The tropical plants failed – coffee, sugar cane, banana – as well as lagerstroemia, liriodendron and lapageria. The garden had only one small area of sandy soil, where fine rooted plants like melaleucas and proteaceae could be persuaded to grow.

The Hanburys took on a head gardener, Ludwig Winter, who had been working at the Tuileries but had been sacked by the Empress Eugénie for singing 'La Marseillaise'. He stayed at La Mortola for six years before opening his own nursery in Bordighera, where he bred *Acacia hanburyana*, the highly successful Riviera florists' mimosa. He too became another source of plants for the garden. In 1869 Thomas returned to China for two years, leaving Daniel in charge of the garden with Mr Winter. When he returned for good, he was a married man, and brought back from Japan a *Cycas revoluta*, the Sacred Palm, and a baby son, Cecil.

As important as the plants themselves, were the understanding and appreciation of the cultures of the countries from which they came. During his Japanese travels Thomas had become interested in Shintoism, a religion in which nature is venerated. This, combined

LEFT: THE FOUR SEASONS TEMPLE AND CYPRESS AVENUE THAT LEADS TO THE SEA AT LA MORTOLA.

BELOW: DETAIL FROM A BENCH MADE OF PORTLAND STONE, WHICH DOROTHY HANBURY BROUGHT FROM THE TERRACE AT KINGSTON MAURWARD.

with his own Quaker commitment to philanthropy and education, prompted him to open the garden to the public twice a week and 'encourage others in their love of nature'. In recognition of his contribution to Shanghai, the Chinese Ambassador, a personal friend, came to La Mortola to bestow upon Thomas the charm 'Fu', which means happiness and long life. The emblem can still be seen, carved in marble over the entrance gates. Sadly the blessing did not extend to Daniel. Stricken with jaundice and typhoid fever the year after he published his most illustrious work, *Pharmacographia*, he died in England at the age of forty-nine. *Pharmacographia* became the world's standard reference work for the origins of all contemporary drugs.

After Daniel's tragically premature death the garden he had infused with so much life, with so much promise, became his memorial. The momentum he had unleashed now continued unchecked. Seeds, roots and cuttings arrived daily, and each new arrival raised the same question: would it survive? Could it be successfully acclimatized? 'Never go against nature' was Thomas's golden rule, which meant giving each plant the optimum conditions; that is, those most closely resembling its native habitat. By 1893, Sir Joseph Hooker was referring to the collection as unrivalled. The first of many *Hortus Mortolensis* was published three years after Daniel's death in 1875, listing five hundred and fifty-seven species on the seed list, and by 1912 there were five thousand eight hundred species in cultivation.

In 1903 Ellen Willmott persuaded the now Sir Thomas to give the Royal Horticultural Society the site for Wisley Garden in Surrey and established a special relationship between the two gardens. A frequent visitor to La Mortola, she was so excited by what she saw that she started her own garden across the bay at Boccanegra in Latte. Later that year, eighty-one-year-old Canon Henry Ellacombe, another friend of Miss Willmott, provided a rare personal glimpse of the garden. Prior to his arrival he wrote from Nice: 'Detained by a few days' illness aggravated by the mosquitos. I lost my umbrella, I lost my money, and have not recovered either.' His mood soon improved when Sir Thomas and Lady Hanbury greeted him personally at Menton Garavan station. 'I cannot describe the beauty of the position of La Mortola or the charms of the house.' The latter included a 'Chinese painting of a rich blue tree peony, which the Chinese ambassador assures Sir Thomas is a reality but very rare. My bedroom is lovely; one window looks upon

ANOTHER VIEW OF LA MORTOLA.

the mountain and the other on the sea, and no mosquitos. In the morning walked in the garden with Sir Thomas, exceptionally beautiful, every yard full of interest, saw plants of which I may have read but have never seen. The whole place was full of flowers, but I think the speciality of the garden is the wonderful collection of Cape succulents. The aloes were a revelation to me. They were of every size and of every colour, and were for the most part suggestive of kniphofias of the most brilliant colours. I had no idea such things existed. Part of the garden is still in its wild rocky state and it was delightful to me to see growing wild things which are among my chief treasures at Bitton . . . . The walk by the shore was most beautiful, *Cineraria maritima* very abundant.

THE 'FU' EMBLEM OF
HAPPINESS AND LONGEVITY
WAS PRESENTED TO SIR
THOMAS HANBURY BY THE
CHINESE AMBASSADOR. IT
STILL DECORATES THE
ENTRANCE TO THE GARDEN.

It's a stiff walk up and down, but I am not the worse for it.'

For the last twenty-eight years of his life, Thomas spent most of his time at La Mortola, deeply involved in botanical and philanthropic pursuits, sponsoring schools and a hospital and erecting fountains in the village. In Ventimiglia he planted avenues of palms, plane trees and paulownias, and donated the land for the first public garden, as well as endowing the University of Genoa with a department devoted to Ligularian studies. The novelist Arnold Bennett, with whom he lunched in 1904, described him as 'The Lord God of these parts. Sir Thomas has the finest private garden in the world, a hundred acres, five thousand species (some absolutely unique) and forty-six gardeners.' Augustus Hare described it as 'as beautiful as anything out of *Arabian Nights*', and people clamoured for admission. At first it was opened by written request only, and then by 1897 'on days notified by the Mentone hotels'. When Thomas died in 1907, after a short illness, seven thousand people followed his funeral procession from La Mortola to San Remo, where he was cremated. His ashes were buried in his garden at the top of the Cypress Alley.

After Thomas's death, the garden fell largely into the hands of its curator, Alwin Berger, and notable additions included a substantial collection brought back by E.H. Wilson from a two-year visit to China. Dr Brunnthaler also sent back a large collection from his 1909–10 plant-hunting expedition to South Africa, which was detailed in the comprehensive and informative *Hortus Mortolensis* of 1912.

After the outbreak of the First World War, the garden was left untended and overgrown; thousands of plants were lost, and Sir Thomas's widow, Kathleen Hanbury, understandably never returned. When her son Cecil took up the garden again in the 1920s, he endowed a local orphanage in memory of his mother. The garden they returned to was described by his wife Dorothy as 'bare, arid, whitish soil, weed choked plants, innumerable labels and stunted malformed trees and shrubs reminiscent of hospitals just left' – full of amputees.

Sir Cecil and Lady Dorothy installed electricity in the palazzo and went to work on the garden. While preserving its botanical interest, they added an aesthetic touch to what had once been a bachelor's paradise. For help and inspiration they sought the advice of their Cap Ferrat neighbour, the Duke of Connaught. The son of an earlier sketching guest, Queen Victoria, the Duke was the most popular member of royalty on the Riviera, much respected for the interest he took in local affairs. He would arrive every New Year with ideas and suggestions for new plants. The architectural improvements Lady Dorothy and her husband made to La Mortola were inspired by Harold Peto's principles of good design and harmony between house and garden, and his brilliant use of colour which they went to study at Villa Maryland on Cap Ferrat.

Dorothy Hanbury, having grown up near to La Mortola, had known Sir Thomas as a child and was completely dedicated to the garden. She totally rejected the idea of having 'a Riviera garden' as being something too new, vulgar even, and sought to surround the sixteenth-century palazzo with features from Italian Renaissance gardens. Thus they straightened the 'wiggly' paths into long vistas and formal steps; and introduced pools, splashing fountains, and stone statues and seats. Dorothy was able to deploy and combine the talents of her father, J.F. Symons Jeune, a landscape gardener, and her brother, Captain Symons Jeune, the rock garden designer. Her father made a main axis through the centre of the garden, called Viale Nuovo, and this was planted on either side with wide borders of *Echium fastuosum*, flanked by double rows of almond trees punctuated by old olive jars. On a semi-circular flight of steps they planted a mass of pink 'Sinica' roses and the single white Anemone rose, with tall double pink Japanese cherries behind, and weeping standard wisterias hanging over the walls. Her father died in 1925, but her brother continued the work, adding three circular flights of steps towards the top of the Viale Nuovo – now the backbone of the garden.

Three very charming little *giardinetti*, small terraces built of Roman bricks, were designed by Dorothy Hanbury herself as cool, shady spring gardens, all connected by very steep, nearly spiral flights of steps. The top terrace had rosy tree peonies and judas trees surrounded by a hedge of cypresses clipped into arches (also found in the gardens of Edith Wharton and Humphrey Waterfield). Inside, there was a

THE ASPARAGUS-LIKE AGAVES, ALOES THAT FLOWER ONCE AND THEN DIE, AND THE TOWERING CANARY PALMS WERE COMPLETELY 'TAKEN FOR GRANTED' BY THE HANBURY CHILDREN. THEY EXCITE GREAT CURIOSITY IN THE YOUNGSTERS WHO NOW VISIT THE GARDEN.

paved circle of thin Roman bricks surrounded with rows of Madonna lilies in pots, standing like ghosts beneath the dark hedges. The second terrace was a blaze of orange dimorphotheca and marigolds, double orange and scarlet nasturtiums, with brownish-red leaves and single deep scarlet flowers – a flamboyant use of orange that was probably inspired by Peto's Villa Maryland. The third and lowest terrace was shaded by palm and lemon trees, with a cool seat and a few Roman statues. Through it runs a pergola draped with *Clematis armandii*, with Madonna lilies lining both sides of the path.

Dorothy Hanbury gave the garden structure and her plantings were exuberant. She loved colour and used it boldly in 'riotous masses', responding sensually like an artist to the baking heat, the virulent and startling colours of the sea, the light and the scents. 'In front of the house, below the terrace wall, lie two scented gardens: the Upper Winter Terrace has fragrant borders of dark brown wall flowers, thyme, rosemary, scented geraniums, lemon scented eucalyptus (kept low for easy picking of the scented leaves) and tobacco flowers; directly below, the Lower Winter Terrace is covered with brick-red bougainvillaea and a row of formal orange trees bordering the path.'

Dorothy gathered and grouped together the sub-tropical plants, the succulents and Australian plants which had been distributed all over the garden, and underplanted them with sheets of flowering bulbs such as *Tulipa clusiana, Tulipa praecox, Anemone fulgens*, sparaxis and isias of many colours, turning it into an aesthetic as well as a botanical spectacle.

At the bottom of the garden, where the soil is richer through being washed down from above, lay the kitchen garden and vineyard. The latter produced light heady wine from Muscat grapes – 'that will not travel,' Dorothy reported, 'even as far as Menton by car'. From the extensive citrus collection they made candied fruits; the rind was so thick it had to be boiled continuously in sea water for three weeks, then for another three in sugar, with further large quantities of each being added every day. The Second World War ended this, and very nearly ended the garden itself. Bombs aimed at the important Corniche road, which bordered the top of La Mortola, sometimes missed their target and blew up parts of the garden instead; meanwhile the palazzo, requisitioned by the Italian army, became an officers' mess – in every sense of the word.

Dorothy returned after the war, a widow, to face appalling destruction for the second time. Her imposing six foot three inch frame directed a diminished fleet of gardeners, and as the garden became more and more of a financial burden and more difficult to manage she was dealt two severe blows; one to the garden, by the devastating winter of 1955, another the following year to herself, when an accident on the front terrace confined her permanently to a wheelchair. It was shortly after this that Winston Churchill came to La Mortola for the first time. Having lunched at Mortola village with Wendy and Emery

SPLENDID CONVOLVULUS
FLORIDUS FROM THE
CANARIES WITH THE RECENTLY
RESTORED PALAZZO IN THE
BACKGROUND.

Reves, he felt 'inspired to visit his wife's favourite house'. There he found 'the charming Lady Hanbury' in her wheelchair, and wrote to Clementine about it. 'She had *not* known of your visits though this would have delighted her. She knows you from of old. You did not tell me she had offered to lend you her house and grounds in 1945 but we were about to start for Marrakech . . . I clambered up to the square terrace and we all sat and talked. She had sent her conveyance. It was Queen Victoria's Special Chair, in which I was wheeled about from the top to the bottom (the sea) and the bottom to the top, and saw everything, accompanied by the whole family. It is indeed a wonderful spot.'

Dorothy was no longer able to maintain La Mortola, and developers were closing in for the kill. However, rather than allowing the promontory to be divided, in 1960 she sold it to the Italian Government on the understanding that it would be maintained as a garden and centre for botanical study. She then retired to live in the Casa Nirvana, a bachelor guesthouse, where she died in 1971.

La Mortola thus passed into the hands of the Italians, upon whose soil it stood – the countrymen of Marco Polo, the emissary and traveller whom Sir Thomas had immortalized in a dazzling gold mosaic in the porch of the palazzo. The porch, as Canon Ellacombe had noted on his visit, used to be filled with an abundance of cut flowers for visitors to take away – the essence of the Hanbury philosophy.

Cecil Hanbury had already forged links with the Italians in 1927, when he instigated a student exchange programme between Kew and

La Mortola. As a result two young Italian gardeners who had been trained at Kew became head gardeners at La Mortola. So successful was this exchange that Kew Gardens expanded the practice, to include other botanical gardens throughout the world.

After their initial enthusiasm, the Italian authorities began to regard the gardens as more of a liability than an asset. At the mercy of bureaucrats and philistines who thought the costs too great and the return too small, the gardens were severely starved of funds. At one point, the gardeners weren't paid for a year and the curator Pier Giorgio Campodonico had to conduct his correspondence by replying on the back of the letters he had received. Storms of international, especially English, protests eventually produced results. Total restoration of the palazzo, terraces, *giardinetti* and paths has now been completed, and the replacement and enrichment of the famous collections is under way under the energetic and imaginative direction of Professor Paula Profumo. Meanwhile the visitors continue to pour in, forty thousand of them every year. The shrieks and excited chatter of boisterous school-children echo through the eucalyptus glades and citrus groves; they stare with curiosity at the marble memorials to the Hanbury family, wondering who these Englishmen were. Daniel Hanbury was never happier, it is said, than when showing children the arcane curiosities of his garden in Clapham.

BOCCANEGRA

ELLEN WILLMOTT

The granddaughter of a Southwark chemist and friend of the Hanburys, Ellen Willmott was born into a charmed life. From her mother she inherited a love of plants, from her godmother £1,000 on every birthday, and from her father the means to buy as many plants and hire as many gardeners as she liked. By the time the money had finally run out she had blazed a trail of horticultural glory from Essex to the South of France Boccanegra was her Waterloo.

ELLEN WILLMOTT, AN ACCOMPLISHED PHOTOGRAPHER, IS HERE CAPTURED IN OILS.

Since the age of nine Ellen had raised the seeds sent from New Zealand by her uncle, a botanist and horticulturalist, whose own garden unfortunately was to disappear under volcanic ash. As a botanist she was largely self-taught. Her intellect would have fitted her for a more rigorous education, but at the time, only Cambridge admitted women, and all the Willmotts traditionally went to Oxford. With an academic background she could have gone further in her experimental work with cultivars – the aspect that most absorbed her. As it was, her great opus, *The Genus Rosa*, written in twenty-five instalments from 1910 to 1914 and illustrated by Alfred Parsons, stretched her to breaking point; never more sorely did she rue her lack of formal botanic training and she never wrote professionally again.

In 1872, after the death of her youngest daughter

Ada, Mrs Willmott moved to Warley Place in Essex. Here she laid out the thirty-three-acre garden along the revolutionary ideas of William Robinson, planting bulbs in drifts – the estate children were instructed to fling them from their wheelbarrows. A hundred and fifty thousand species and hybrids thrived under her care at Warley. Remarkably versatile as a hybridizer, she produced good results with narcissi and daffodils. Recipients of seed lists were requested to return their results in Latin so she could understand them all – even those from Eastern European countries. The index seminum was printed by a press that she had assembled herself. She also operated her own darkroom and became an accomplished ivory carver and wood turner.

It was Ellen Willmott's mother who first led her abroad. Severely rheumatic and now confined to a bath chair and donkey chaise, she sought relief in the spas of Europe; her favourite being Aix les Bains in the Savoie at the foot of the Alps. The mountains may have inspired Ellen's first exercise in landscape design: the alpine garden at Warley – a tableau complete with an imported alpine hut which arrived fully equipped – and it certainly inspired her enough to want to garden there. She bought Château de Tresserve, which later became famous for its collection of irises and over eleven thousand roses, and which acted as a stepping stone to the Riviera. She had already paid several visits to the Hanbury's garden at La Mortola which opened a whole new world for her. To observe a new climate and to have a fresh terrain on which to experiment with indigenous Mediterranean flora as well as sub-tropical and exotic plants, was a prospect she found as compelling as the potato trials she had conducted earlier at Warley, when she had grown every known variety – purely out of curiosity.

Within a few years she could no longer resist possessing her own patch of scorched earth. It was probably Sir Thomas Hanbury who found the spot for her, two miles along the coast to the east of La Mortola, in Latte. Boccanegra was a twenty-one-acre olive grove with optimum conditions for growing exotic plants: hot, dry, south-facing, and sloping steeply to the sea. The house, set high at the top of the garden, flush with what was once a country lane, is now blackened by fumes from a roaring stream of traffic. It was a great pity that Sir Thomas died only two years later, his inspiration was much missed, and Lady Hanbury subsequently wrote to say how much he too had valued their friendship.

By the time she bought Boccanegra in 1905 she was one of only two female recipients of the Victoria Medal – the other being Gertrude Jekyll. Jekyll had had to collect the awards for both of them, as Miss Willmott was busy gardening at Tresserve. As she explained to her friend and mentor, the director of Harvard's Arnold Arboretum: 'My plants and my gardens come before anything in life for me, and all my time is given up to working in one garden or another, and when it is too dark to see the plants themselves, I read or write about them.' Plants were her real passion and she always had more success growing seeds and cuttings received from various expeditions than even Kew Gardens or Harvard's Arboretum.

In tackling the garden Ellen Willmott first addressed the problem of irrigation. She channelled the spring and autumn downpours through natural water courses which led to huge concrete reservoirs. These

AT THE BOTTOM OF THE GARDEN LIES THE POTAGER, AND VISIBLE IN THE BACKGROUND IS THE RAILWAY LINE THAT MISS WILLMOTT FOUND SO IRKSOME.

tanks are still in use today, and are perhaps her greatest contribution. Aiming at a wild botanical garden along the lines of La Mortola, she laid out the paths in a William Robinson kind of way, following contours and the natural gaps between rocks. Unfortunately there are no surviving plans, but the broad scheme can be gleaned from the rust-proof metal labels which remain, hinting at collections of numbered plants and supplying clues that there may have been a rock garden inspired by her neighbour, the alpine specialist Sybille Campbell. Stone benches were posted in strategic spots, which she used for resting, admiring the view and, naturally, recording her observations.

The main-line railway track which runs along the rocky shoreline at the bottom of the garden, before disappearing into a tunnel, became an obsessive source of irritation for her. Some years earlier, her neighbour at Warley Place, Count Lescher, had built two cottages in an adjacent field, which she felt ruined her perfect alpine picture. So abusive had she become then that the Count threatened to shoot her. This time at Boccanegra she took on the Ferrovie Italiane, who repossessed her land to stop her growing trees too near the track. Ellen being an accomplished linguist, a colourful and heated argument ensued – to no avail. Her appetite for a good fight was such that many years later, in her obituary in the *Gardeners' Chronicle*, it was said that she had given the injunction 'love your enemies' a new meaning because she had obviously 'got so much enjoyment out of them'.

Another thing not done by halves was the ordering of plants, and when the most costly and necessary work on her water supply was completed she spent £2,000 on plants in four years – the same amount that she had paid to purchase Château de Tresserve fifteen years before! She bought figs, opuntias, bignonia and mimosa; citrus and bay; cedars, eleagnus and yuccas; pittosporum and *Mahonia aquifolium* by the hundred; three hundred cannas, six hundred *tulipa clusiana*, and aloes and agaves by the dozen.

Ellen Willmott kept her finger on the pulse of each of her three comprehensive botanical gardens by means of hundreds of postcards. No plant was committed to the soil without her specific instructions, and for each of these establishments (which she visited twice a year) she paid all the bills and ran the houses and households as well. A year after purchasing Boccanegra she began to borrow money. Shunting a substantial household the length and breadth of France by train proved expensive, so she bought herself 'a chain-driven Charron car, complete with black Mozambiquan chauffeur and his white French wife'. They made a picturesque pair and slotted well into village life. In each of her properties Miss Willmott was fortunate to have excellent and dedicated head gardeners, for when her fortune began to dwindle they barely received sufficient wages to keep them ticking over. Even her friend William Robinson marvelled at her spending, observing that the shortest road to ruin was to own several houses.

In an effort to keep afloat she leased Boccanegra for several years to Lady Menzies who, sadly, took no

HUGE OCTOPUS-LIKE VARIEGATED AGAVE.

interest in the garden. Faced with bankruptcy, and as a last hope she offered to sell the property to her friend Alice de Rothschild. 'Why not sell a picture?' replied the pragmatic Alice. When finally, in 1920, she had been forced to part with both her French houses, she told Alice she would never go abroad again. True to her word, she returned to Warley, where she became a somewhat Bohemian figure, rising at dawn with trowel and trug; weeding and planting in an old brown serge skirt and jacket and wooden sabots. The excitement and magic of her gardens never left her, and she died at the age of seventy-six, a true Patroness of Plants. 'Willmottiae', 'warleyensis' or 'Miss Willmott' are her legacies, many named after her gratefully by the nurseries she sponsored. Her best-known plant is probably 'Miss Willmott's Ghost', *Eryngium giganteum*, whose seeds she is said to have sprinkled in the gardens she visited.

Her butler said of Miss Willmott: 'There was nothing my lady could not do.' There is also a most endearing image of her in Audrey Le Lievre's vivid biography where she is described as 'returning from one of her many long walks, her knapsack bulging with plants acquired from friends, with as much soil as she could carry or dared ask for'.

Boccanegra now belongs to Guido Piacenza. He and his brothers inherited it in 1983 from their mother, who had owned it since 1956. Like Miss Willmott, Guido is a plantsman. His interest is in the plants themselves, which is rather unusual for an Italian. His father was a friend of Harold Hillier, and in 1966 he bought Hillier's magnificent collection of

BOCCANEGRA HAS THAT QUINTESSENTIAL, LUMINOUS RIVIERA LIGHT AND THESE EUCALYPTUS BRANCHES SEEM TO FLOAT ON AIR.

51

rhododendrons and other species from Genoa and planted it both in his garden in Pollone and in the public park he had donated to the town. Until 1968, when his father died, Guido had been an avid bird collector. Two weeks touring English gardens with Hillier, who showed him all the best cultivars, trees and plants, changed his life. He returned to Italy and let all his birds out of the aviary. It hit him like a bolt, he said: suddenly, plants were the thing. He began with conifers, then hardy plants, then tender ones.

Guido maintains Boccanegra as a private botanical garden, respecting its character and planting judiciously with Mediterranean, Australian and South African plants, which do well. Tropical plants requiring moisture or humidity do not. New additions include unusual bulbs from Holland, *Petrea volubilis*, *Cycas circinalis*, *Beaumontia grandiflora*, *Polygala virgata* and *Nierembergia caerulea*. Miss Willmott's greatest successes had been her rock garden and succulent area, and the *Agathis australis*, *Yucca australis* and *Arbutus andrachnoides*.

Does the ghost of Miss Willmott still inhabit Boccanegra? Some of her plants have survived because they were given a good start. All that remains of her once enormous collection of irises and pelargoniums (many of which she gave to La Mortola) are a few pelargoniums, and *Iris unguicularis*. It is so dry, and the competition from the roots of the larger trees and olives so overwhelming, that only cacti and succulents thrive without assistance. Guido shares Miss Willmott's ideological approach and, like her, he regards his work as a mission in life. For Guido, gardens are like art – and should be above commercial considerations. He feels gardens should be subsidized like museums. Independently wealthy through his family's prestigious textile business, he has been able to underwrite his specialist nursery, which has a very good list including many old-fashioned roses. Enthusiasts, amateurs and professionals alike come to see his unique collection of tender and tropical plants, but more often than not his clientele want something large and evergreen which will flower all year round. He supplies many of the more interesting gardens but in Italy there isn't the demand for rare plants which exists in England. Guido's ideal would be to have no customers at all, but at the same time he needs to balance his books and make his nursery pay. Meanwhile, at Boccanegra, where his young son Felice, he says, is the fastest growing 'plant', Guido waits for rain.

THE WILD GARDEN LOOKING EAST TOWARDS A CAREFULLY SITED URN. ORIGINALLY IN HUMPHREY'S ESSEX GARDEN, WILLIAM BOUGHT IT FROM THE NEW OWNER AND BROUGHT IT TO THE CLOS.

CLOS DU PEYRONNET

THE WATERFIELDS

Three generations of Waterfields have gardened at the Clos du Peyronnet, and each has made an aspect of it his own. For William Waterfield the garden is his life. He has been described as the last of his breed, the last English plantsman on the Riviera. He celebrated his fiftieth birthday on 29 July 1992 by throwing a party with a thousand candles illuminating the garden. The Clos is the only remaining English enclave in a quarter of Menton that was once almost entirely British. Within its walls the traditions, ideas and courtesies of an English plantsman are enacted daily, while the customs and the friendships offered by his adopted country are also valued.

The choice of Menton originated with William's grandmother, Barbara Waterfield, a great *malade imaginaire*, who could bear neither the climate of India, where her husband Derick had had a brilliant career in the Civil Service, nor that of England, to which he retired. In 1915 they bought an Italianate villa in which to overwinter. Built in 1896 from the remains of an old farmhouse, it was set in an acre of terraced olives, its walled boundaries punctuated by cypresses. Very close to the Italian border on one side, and Katherine Mansfield's little villa Isola Bella on the other, the Clos du Peyronnet is named after the valley in which it stands, its garden initially all Victorian bedding and palms.

A few years later, the family left their English home for good and settled permanently in France. Their two sons, Anthony and Humphrey, commuted to Eton on the famous *Train Bleu* – boarding it at the Garavan stop, close to the house, and alighting the following day at Victoria Station. Humphrey went on to read history at Oxford, and although his father would have liked him to follow a career in the diplomatic service, he wanted to be a painter. His father promised to support him for a year, but only if he was awarded a First. He earned himself a congratulatory First, studied art at the Ruskin School, and then took up the life of a young artist. He had however, remained very attached, as one does, to the English garden of his early youth. He went some way to recapturing his memories permanently by buying four acres of what had once been the rubbish tip of the village of Broxted in Essex, to be near the home of Nancy Tennant, his lifelong companion. Here he built a unique garden around a very modern house, designed by Ernest Goldfinger, and called it Hill Pasture. However, he continued to visit the Clos, and travelled extensively in Italy, while cutting his 'gardening teeth' in England.

Hill Pasture was much in the Hidcote style because, together with Lawrence Johnston, he was a friend of Norah Lindsay. 'Good plants well shown' was Humphrey's dictum, and his skill lay in combining wonderful and unusual exotic plants with good design. 'The plants were an eclectic lot. What took his fancy. He was a very original and innovative man, enthusiastic, extravagant, great fun; what is known in Provençal as *bien typé*: a strong personality which, as one gets into one's stride in life, becomes more assertive,' explains his nephew William Waterfield. 'He had a natural bent for designing gardens and should have pursued it, but felt it was rather beneath him, that he was a painter and should be painting; that painting was a noble art and garden designing rather third rate, which was a pity because he was more talented as a garden designer than a painter. He seldom sold his pictures nor made much effort to do so.'

Barbara and Derick Waterfield died just before the Second World War, leaving the Clos to their two sons. Humphrey was thirty-nine years old and very keen to take it on and keep it going, because he had grown up there, whereas Anthony, more of a businessman, was less

ABOVE: HUMPHREY AND ANTHONY WITH THEIR MOTHER BARBARA WATERFIELD AT THE CLOS.

RIGHT: THE CYPRESS ARCH PATH LEADS TO THE EAST BOUNDARY WALL, DECORATED WITH A MEDUSA'S HEAD. CATCHING THE LIGHT IS SENECIO PETASITES.

THE LONG PERGOLA, A
CENTRAL ELEMENT IN THE
GARDEN'S DESIGN AND THE
SITE OF MANY CONVIVIAL
MEALS. ARUM LILIES,
CAMELLIA AND CYCLAMEN
PERSICUM ARE IN VIEW.

attached. But Menton had been bombed and shelled; Italian troops had requisitioned the house, and the garden lay totally neglected, so all in all it wasn't considered to be worth very much. Anthony agreed to keep it going – but it was a luxury. With no land to sell off to raise capital, the house was split into flats with separate entrances, and rented out.

From 1946 until his death in 1971, Humphrey spent every winter at the Clos, applying his talents as painter, landscape designer, plantsman and gardener to the fabric of the garden, whose structure he embellished with vistas, ornaments and plants. Each of the three generations has made its own contribution to the infrastructure of the garden. The gradual installation and modernization of the irrigation systems and the strengthening of terrace walls has been an ongoing operation.

Keen on surprises, Humphrey created vistas in which there is 'a lot more than initially meets the eye', observes William. The most sophisticated of these is in the orchard. It works in two directions and changes focus with distance. At the very top of the garden was an irregularly shaped pool of water always known as 'the black pool'. Looking down over the terraces to the sea must have given him the idea of putting a pool on each of the four intervening levels. This much-admired feature, inspired by the Villa d'Este at Tivoli, was always known as his Water Staircase.

Beauty was paramount in Humphrey's life, and money only important in that it could provide a new urn or statue for the garden – which echoes an aphorism attributed to Cole Porter's prep school teacher:

that there was always enough money in life, never enough beauty. Because he made no effort to sell his paintings, there were inevitably financial constraints: the Water Staircase was strictly a one *bassin* a year project. Friends arrived clutching the meagre £50 one was allowed to prise from English soil in those days and were whisked off to Lorenzi the *maçon*, creator of the Scala Nobile (a stone staircase), and the Water Staircase, so that work could continue. The Cypress Alley, which also drew its inspiration from Italy, is technically quite tricky to achieve. The cypresses are allowed to grow until they reach the right height, and are then tied together at the top and clipped into shape – impossible in a windy place because they simply pull apart.

At the top of the garden, 'Humph' built an aviary, the idea being that it should look completely natural. On opening the door one followed stepping-stones through a magic wood, with lovely tropical birds fluttering around. 'But in practice,' says William, 'every time the wind blew and the trees waved, holes appeared and the birds flew out, so it was never a great success.' For the last sixteen years, until recently, it was inhabited by a scraggy old cock.

Friends and neighbours made contributions to the garden, which were recorded in Humphrey's gardening book. From Norah Warre at Villa Roquebrune in the spring of 1959, *Rosa gigantea*; from Maybud Campbell in 1963, *Akebia quinata* – both plants still extant; but the *Bryophylum* from Basil Leng, sadly, died. Charles de Noailles was a chum,

A SPRINGTIME VIEW OF THE WATER STAIRCASE WITH AMARYLLIS BELLADONNA HYBRIDS, SPANISH BLUEBELLS, MALUS LEMOINEI AND KNIPHOFIA SPECIES.

and never visited anyone without bringing a plant. From Lawrence Johnston, at Serre de la Madone, came *Mahonia siamensis*. The year after 'Johnnie' died, Humphrey's entry in his diary read, 'Spring. 1959. Johnnie Johnston's year. Pots. Cherubs. Stone seat.' Nancy Lindsay had inherited La Madone, and unable to finance it, sold the house and grounds separately from the garden ornaments. They turned up everywhere, the Anduze vases recognizable by an intertwined 'LJ'. Maybud Campbell and Humphrey bought some, we know, and Humphrey purchased the stone seat placed at the top of the garden, with *'Viva Il Duce'* carved in it – a relic from the war. He used the pots to accentuate vistas on a landscape which then still existed. His back, he said, never recovered from carrying the pots.

Humphrey used to go home to Essex for the spring and summer, and during the 1950s and 60s, increasingly appreciated for his taste and knowledge, was commissioned to design, among others, gardens at Abbots Ripton Hall and Grey's Court, near Henley. His style was characterized by the use of grey foliage plants, white, pinks, and the palest of yellows. In the summer his nephew came to stay. To William the arrangement between 'Humph' and 'Aunt Nan' (Nancy Tennant) seemed a wonderful kind of dual life. She lived nearby and came round for lunch, bringing veal and ham pie, and they'd all spend the afternoon together. William and Humphrey gardened. 'Painting was the core of Humphrey's life, far more important than plants or people,' says Nancy Tennant. 'It was always a disappointment to him that any success that came his way was from his gardens rather than his pictures.' In 1971, he was killed in a car accident. William was then nearly thirty.

'I have a very clear memory of what I think of as being my first evening here, having driven from Paris where we lived then, and being allowed out and told I could play in the grotto with my tin soldiers; and being struck by how suddenly the darkness came, instead of the long northern evenings, and being very concerned about this. In my memory the garden has always been the way it is – I remember learning to swim in the *bassin* just above the long *bassin*.'

Once again the garden's future hung in the balance, the family tempted by developers offering large sums to demolish the house and build a block of flats. William, meanwhile, had read botany at Eton and Oxford, travelled to the United States on a PhD course, worked on the Oxford English Dictionary at Oxford, and for a pharmaceutical firm in Kent. In Oxford he had a 'two up two down' in Jericho and put a huge effort into its tiny garden. He saw the Clos as an exciting opportunity, a nice way to live – 'I have always accepted things as they come,' he says – and went on to make the Clos his permanent home.

The old gardener Mario Lavagna had been there since the 1920s and had kept the garden going; a 'prop and stay' between Humphrey's death and William's arrival. There is a plaque in the garden commemorating his tenure. He was Italian, but born in Antibes, and came to the Clos as a boy. Apart from service in the First World War and deportation, like all the Italians in Menton, during the Second World War, he spent his whole life there. He certainly had his own way of doing things when he first started, but when William came in

HUMPHREY WATERFIELD'S
SELF-PORTRAIT.

1976, Mario had been working for the same English family for fifty years and had had time to adjust. William remembers him as a sweet, gentle man.

From Mario, William learned to dead-head the nolina with a saw on a long pole, and he still dead-heads the yuccas, which are twenty to thirty feet high. The palms, however, are now trimmed professionally. 'I've had enough of standing beneath a shower of rat and pigeon droppings and an eight-foot palm frond with vicious six-inch spines whistling past my neck.'

William has been described as a '*collecteur acharné*' which he defines as 'wanting to collect every known salvia species in the world, some five or six hundred different species. After a while you realize this is folly, this is madness – if you've got twenty salvias you've probably got enough. I collect for the sake of collecting, absolutely, I do. I'm quite interested in having the French national collection of *romulea* and *chasmanthe*. There are only four *chasmanthe* in the world and I have them all – nobody else here has – and all correctly named, which is important. They are South Africans, very well adapted to the South of France and the Mediterranean region and should be encouraged for that reason. In *romulea* (tiny bulbs known as cape crocuses), I'm aware that Maurice Boussard, the grand old man of iridaceae, probably has the best collection in Europe, but if he's not interested in having the national collection, I would like to have it. The French organization seems rather sleepy and I've got rather bored with their inactivity. Perhaps

A JUDAS TREE AND ACANTHUS ENCIRCLE A SIX-HUNDRED YEAR OLD OLIVE IN THE WILD GARDEN.

bulbous genera are not what they want.'

His interest in bulbs developed naturally from living in a climate to which they are particularly suited. 'You start with a few, get excited about them, and want more. Bulbs have glorious, wonderful flowers, the size of the flower is quite often out of proportion to the size of the bulb and the whole plant. One of the things I think is smashing and gets me every time is the fact that you start with this scruffy, dried-up little thing with rush-like leaves and it just burgeons and produces a wonderful, great huge flower, not huge like a lotus but huge in relation to the leaves, and then goes back to being this dried-up thing. With a bulb each individual flower is a gem. There are people who are fascinated by Tillandsia. I cannot understand how anyone can get excited about hanging Florida moss, but they would say that Florida moss is fantastic and bulbs are boring.'

Two of his French neighbours approach collecting in ways which puzzle William. Freddie Braun, who was Maybud Campbell's head gardener, is an avid collector of exotic plants, who says that he gets interested in a different thing every year. 'I have very strong feelings about this,' protests William. 'One year it's bamboos with him, the next year it's palms. I can't understand it at all that he should throw out all the bamboos he collected last year and start collecting palms, and the next year he throws out the palms and starts collecting something else. That's his attitude.' Freddie only throws out a plant 'if I find one rarer than the one I've got', but William doesn't go for that. 'I think one should have common things if they appeal to you, if they look wonderful. Just to be rare is not enough. After all,' he argues, 'Kew can grow, at a latitude of 40 or so, all sorts of tropical things because they have the right greenhouses with extra lighting – potentially you can grow anything anywhere really, and so what?

'I also feel very strongly about my neighbour Arnoult, who lives in our old gardener's cottage with a little garden, and for six months of the year half his plants are wrapped up in plastic. Well, who wants to walk out into a garden in which everything is wrapped up in plastic? One of the delights and charms of this lovely, smashing, salubrious climate in the South of France is that the winter is just as exciting and favourable to vegetation as the summer, often more so, and you can go out into the garden and enjoy wonderful exciting things from South Africa, or Chile or California from November to April. In England, the winter is so miserable that if your garden is wrapped in plastic, it doesn't matter – you aren't going to go out there anyway – but here you can enjoy it all the year round. Having rare plants is not the be-all and end-all.

'A garden should have ninety per cent bones – plants capable of surviving nature's vicissitudes; and only ten per cent that are not hardy; so that you have the structure and the bones to carry on from season to season, and if something dies, nobody notices. I'm always planting more things than I can possibly look after. Often I start with three bulbs, then two, then one the year after, and then none.' Success comes with choosing plants from the same Mediterranean climate. Apart from a few evergreens, and a very few summer growers, the bulbs mostly start burgeoning in late summer. Shoots appear above ground and carry on through winter, depending on the species; or grow and die down from early spring to early summer, again depending on species.

Flowering tends to be in autumn or spring, but all through the winter something is in flower. The bulbs in small pots are repotted annually; those in large pots, biennially. Exposed to the elements during growth, the small pots are 'oversummered' on shelving behind the house, protected from rain, while the big pots are left in place but covered by panes of glass if the weather looks threatening. He grows all his bulbs in pots except for the very common or very large ones, unless they are particularly rare like *brunsvigias*, which would otherwise disappear in open ground.

William provides a home for over thirty varieties of sage, and has recently made a new departure into species pelargoniums, which all come from South Africa and are therefore very adaptable to life in Menton. Half of them come from the winter rainfall part of South Africa, and are perfectly suited to the Riviera winter. The other half, from the summer rainfall region, are kept along the veranda, where they are protected from winter rain and can be watered in summer.

Any interesting plant is always welcome to William. He was given an exciting new avocado which nobody else had, called Topa Topa, by his friend Monsieur Deleuze, who lives in Corsica surrounded by a hundred and forty varieties of palm, but in a gardening vacuum – because nobody gardens there. Corsicans are either too poor to have gardens or else are making them on the Riviera and in Provence, so Deleuze has to take a plane to be among 'gardening people'. From the Ville de Menton, there is a new excitement for William – a *Tupidanthus*

VIEW DOWN THE STEPS OF THE WATER STAIRCASE TO THE SEA. MALUS LEMOINEI OVERHANGS THE TOP STEP AND THE CRIMSON FLOWERS CONTRAST WITH THE COLOUR OF THE FISH.

calyptratus, which is relatively rare. From Dino Pellizaro, 'the best nurseryman on the Côte', he got the elegant *Abutilon vitifolium*, which normally doesn't like the area, so Dino grafted it on to a suitable species of abutilon.

People are always asking William for plants which are constantly in flower. 'If you can find the magic plant like *Lantana sellowiana*, which is in flower all the year round, after about four months you just cease to notice it. Half the pleasure is watching something and thinking, "Oh, it'll be out next week", or "It's not as good this week as it was last week". You might as well have plastic flowers dotted around.' The other question people always ask is whether all the pools are connected: does the water run from one pool to the other? He finds it curious that people persistently pose this question, because he doesn't find it of any interest whatsoever. 'Maybe it's something they feel they ought to ask me, like people asking for the name of a plant. My philosophy is that anyone who is a student or a professional is welcome to come, and that they will be fired up. I'm very anti garden visits for people with no interest who come just for a wander round. My uncle was a great one for "encouraging youth".'

With each passing year William feels more at home, more *bien dans sa peau*. He does all the work himself, having just completed a whole new irrigation system as part of his plan to improve the infrastructure, which has held up very well, unlike the nearby Colombières garden, which was badly built and is falling apart. The last occupant of the aviary, the wizened rooster, has finally died. 'He's been here as long as I have,' remarks William mournfully. The fencing has come down and a marsh has been created, making an additional habitat to prolong the garden's flowering season. By topping it up with a hose, he can grow aquatic plants like lotus that will flower in the summer without constant watering.

William Waterfield lives the life of a dedicated English plantsman, taking weekend walks in the country with his Jack Russells Pinky, Polly and Puck. He is an avid garden visitor and an exhibitor at the local flower show, where he won first prize two years in a row. If you exchanged the Basses Alpes for Dorset, and the Fêtes des Plantes in

Nice for the Royal Horticultural Halls, you would almost think he lived in England. He returns there every year for a fortnight's fishing, for English sausages, Melton Mowbray pork pies and croquet. Every Easter Saturday William holds an egg hunt at the Clos for children under ten, who also play traditional English games. The list of games is pinned up by a hunting knife stuck, Swallows and Amazons style, into an enormous *Phoenix canariensis*. It is the sort of thing, he says, that his Aunt Nan used to organize brilliantly, and which makes the garden repay the care one gives it. Similarly, he likes to have people painting in the garden. It's a garden that is lived in; at once comfortable, beautiful and interesting. Designer gardens with 'pine cones in the grate' do not appeal. And what of the French? 'Well,' says William, 'they really perk up if you say something is *comestible*.'

WILLIAM WATERFIELD WITH HIS EXHIBIT OF RARE BULBS AT THE FETE DES PLANTES IN NICE IN 1992, THE YEAR HE WON HIS FIRST CUP.

LA GAROUPE

THE ABERCONWAYS AND THE NORMANS

DATURA AND STRELITZIAS AT
LA GAROUPE.

La Garoupe has been honed to perfection by three generations of the same family and is probably the last place to evoke the Riviera in all its style and glory. This garden, surrounded by a wild, pure and peaceful landscape and sea, have given it a timeless atmosphere: only the style of a yacht gliding past, the speed of an airplane and, within the garden, a jaunty little golf car, licence plate number A-1, give the game away. At the controls is Antony Norman, who, following an operation last year, now whizzes along the gravel paths on wheels. The grandson of Lady Aberconway of Bodnant, who created the garden in 1905, Antony began exploring it as a child of five, with a horse and cart. Each Christmas he would arrive from England on the *Train Bleu* with his brother Willoughby – both of them tucked up in the overhead luggage netting.

Every morning at ten he sets off from the south terrace, sometimes on his own, sometimes with a horticultural group – and a crib of the garden prepared for him by his friend Fleur Champin. What memories these tours must bring back: families, friends, wars; the successes, tragedies and adventures of nearly a century. How profoundly his world has changed, how irreversibly the Riviera has been transformed. One can hardly begin to imagine what it was like when Lady Aberconway settled on this south-eastern tip of Cap d'Antibes after scouring the coast from Monaco to Toulon. She might have bought the whole Cap,

THESE MARBLE STEPS FORM
PART OF THE MAIN AXIS OF
THE GARDEN. DURING THE
WAR, ITALIAN TROOPS ON
HORSEBACK GALLOPED UP
AND DOWN THEM.

but wanted 'just enough land for a nice garden'. The hundred acres certainly provided her with plenty of space, but not very much soil, as it was largely rock. Undaunted, and no doubt to the beat of that well-known drum 'location, location, location', she erected belvedere after belvedere to find the best possible site for the house. Eventually she found it. That very spot is now smack in the middle of the entrance hall on a north–south axis which originates somewhere on the Mont Blanc range, swoops across the Bay of Antibes, through the middle of the château, over the gleaming white terrace, and down the hundred and thirty marble steps to the rocky cove below.

The architects were Ernest George and Yates. 'No individual was ever mentioned by Lady Aberconway, who worked on the plans herself,' Anne Norman points out. 'Certainly no architect ever visited the site, and the work was carried out in feet and inches by a family of Italian builders, whose descendants also built the Tourelle de la Garoupe for us in 1953. They had no modern equipment, not even a cement mixer.' The site of the celebrated south terraces was originally a wilderness of solid rock, and the area had to be blasted to give sufficient depth for the soil, imported from the north side of the château, where it was very fertile. In those days the boundaries stretched to the Bay of Garoupe, and Lady Aberconway ran a commercial nursery in the rich red earth, growing roses and the asparagus fern English gentlemen used to wear in their buttonholes; the entire crop was despatched to England in baskets.

During the early days the garden was tended by fourteen gardeners and ploughed by oxen. Along the road from Opio, which has now vanished under two motorways, a business park and umpteen megastores, a *boeuf* was brought down to La Garoupe, standing on a cart drawn by a second *boeuf*. Exhausted after ploughing the vineyard and gardens for three days he was put back on the cart and pulled home again. The same beasts were used in the olive groves, reputedly planted by the Romans, in which one tree is said to be the oldest on the coast. Antony doesn't grow vegetables in the fertile Esterel soil. 'You can't grow vegetables and flowers together,' his mother had wisely observed, 'because the gardeners put all their energy into the vegetables, which they think more worthwhile.' So as not to tempt fate, only lemons and oranges are grown, from which marmalade is made. La Garoupe once produced its own wine, but Antony describes it as 'rather grim', and the former vineyard now contains roses from the Meilland nursery which is practically on the doorstep. These are used as cut flowers for the house and are grown, like vines, in *rangées*, which allows easy access by tractor for weeding and rotavating. The olives are neither harvested nor pruned. 'They are beautiful trees, and when I see them mutilated in the rest of the country they look simply awful. All I do is lop off the lower branches and the suckers.' Several of the trees have died from honey fungus, but their ancient trunks now support rambling roses and, more recently, the climber solanum. This flowers throughout the season, unlike the roses which are not remontant. Thousands of cyclamen and freesias seed themselves all along the drive – 'better than where I plant them,' notes Antony, ruefully.

Man and nature work together at La Garoupe. Antony is a landscape gardener at heart with a particular affinity for trees. He likes to see cypresses neatly clipped, and employs a specialist at great expense to do this every other year. The Italians, he observes, let them grow straggly, and he feels this spoils their whole effect. At La Garoupe they are planted in the middle distance, so as not to interfere with the magnificent views, or else flush against the house, like the two enormous *Magnolia grandiflora* flanking the front door. 'I was taught quite young by my mother never to resist the temptation to cut down a tree which has been there for many years – it's not a good enough excuse. If a tree doesn't give you anything, cut it down; if it's been planted in the wrong place and overshadows the drawing room, cut it down.

'Anything I plant has to be an improvement to the overall landscape. I'm not a collector of rare shrubs or things that nobody else has, unless they add something to the landscape effect of the garden. Then I will have them at any cost, but not because they are unique. I don't pretend this garden is a horticulturalist's paradise – I'm more interested that it should be an overall paradise and that wherever you look the landscaping is beautiful in its fashion.'

Aesthetic ideas have to be practical. Whereas Lady Aberconway had fourteen gardeners looking after her hundred acres, the present twenty-five-acre garden is maintained by two gardeners, sometimes just one. Antony's cypresses may be expensive to trim, but if he

SIR HENRY AND LADY NORMAN WITH THEIR SON ANTONY ON THE TERRACE OF CHATEAU DE LA GAROUPE.

plants informally around them, the overall effect looks polished. For
the wilder areas, he looked around for a sun lover that didn't have to be
watered and could stand the pounding sun. He found the answer to his
prayers in the cistus genus, whose many varieties he obtained, as he
does all his plants and shrubs, from Hilliers.

The *pièce de résistance* at La Garoupe is the parterre, formerly the
home of unhappy shrub roses, a wilted lawn, scorched under the strong
southern exposure, and some unwanted cypresses, planted too close to
the house. 'I wanted an entirely different idea,' says Antony. Many
years before, he had seen the Piazza del Popolo in Rome. The asym-
metrical pattern of stones obviously made an impression on him, for it
served as a base for the design of the parterre. Thus, the wild plants of
the *maquis* are used – rosemary, santolina and lavender – and rigorously
clipped. This forms the very clever link between brilliantly colourful
upper terraces and the wilderness of rocky *garrigue* beyond. Only the
lavender is allowed to flower, the rosemary and santolina being kept to
more subfusc shades of grey and green.

The family have always been fiercely protective of their gardens.
Bodnant had been given to the National Trust with the proviso that all
the decisions involving the garden would be made solely by the family.
In order to save La Garoupe from the axe of the Inland Revenue, Lady
Norman had to make the sacrifice of leaving England and taking up
domicile abroad. This she did in 1963. She had inherited the château in
1934. When the Second World War was immanent, and anticipating

ABOVE: THIS AVENUE OF
ANCIENT OLIVES IS
UNDERPLANTED WITH IRISES.
HERE THE CHASMANTHE
FLORIBUNDI IS IN
FULL BLOOM.

OPPOSITE: FORMERLY THE SITE
OF THE VINEYARD, THE RICH
RED EARTH OF THE ESTEREL
NOW SUPPORTS ORANGES AND
ROSES. IN THE FOREGROUND
ARE SEEDPODS OF
CHASMANTHE FLORIBUNDI.

enemy occupation, she had all the furniture removed and put into safe storage in Cannes. The château, however, was too conspicuous to be useful to the enemy, and was empty to boot, so the Italian troops lived in the other estate houses and contented themselves with using an enormous painting of a saint in the dining-room for target practice, galloping on horseback up and down the fragile marble steps to the sea, and absolutely devastating the garden by digging trenches through it. Throughout the war the family attempted to maintain the garden with funds sent through Switzerland. Although it was silly to imagine that anyone might land at Garoupe to invade France via a narrow winding road through the jagged rocky mountains of the Esterel, the Germans nevertheless planted over two thousand land mines on the property. Most extraordinary of all was the Norman's Swiss gardener – he said he knew where all the mines were, and gardened around them! After the war, the poor old saint was patched up, the marble steps were repaired and the gardens restored. The mines, meanwhile, were put to good use. After they had been disinterred by German prisoners of war and the detonators removed, the ammonium nitrate charge within was used to fertilize the orange trees.

La Garoupe is a world unto itself, and over the years has stimulated the imaginations of literary geniuses, millionaires and petty thieves alike since Lady Aberconway became one of the first to let her house to summer tenants. Among the more extraordinary of these was blue-haired, yoga-practising Lady Mendl, who brought Cole Porter and his friends Gerald and Sara Murphy – the result of that stay being Villa America. There is a reference in the gardener's memoir from the early 1920s, to the enormously rich widow Mrs Joseph Pulitzer, who took the house for several seasons and entertained magnificently, aided by a huge retinue of servants. She died at Deauville, much regretted by her staff – '*car elle dépensait sans compter!*'

La Garoupe passed sometimes anonymously into literature, as it did on to celluloid, in both films and commercials. It was also the rather poignant location for David Niven's last film, *Three's a Crowd*.

In 1987 the Normans were given golden plants by their friends in celebration of their golden wedding anniversary. Their marriage had begun with a flying honeymoon – just the two of them in his Miles Whitney Straight. Antony was an experienced pilot, and had already raced in the King's Cup, getting into the final in 1935. The year was 1937, Germany was rearming and Churchill ranting, but nobody was taking any notice. In Italy, England was very unpopular because Sir Anthony Eden was being awkward with Mussolini over Abyssinia. Undeterred, the Normans flew down over Venice, to Brioni where no landing place was available. They landed at a 'secret' aerodrome – and were immediately arrested. Brought in front of the station commander, Antony apologized for his unauthorized arrival, explaining, 'I was really trying to go to Brioni', to which the station commander replied, 'That's all right, I'll take you over in my yacht!'

Mrs Norman strode on to the terrace. 'I don't know whether you've noticed,' she announced, 'but our male cycas are extremely excited. It's their year and they are now in full erection and haven't been in three years.' 'Well, it has been a very good year for growth,' added her husband with a twinkle in his eye. 'Plenty of rain in March.'

THE GAROUPE PARTERRE IS A SEA OF GREY AND BLUE.

VILLA ROQUEBRUNE

NORAH WARRE

The extraordinary thing about Villa Roquebrune is that it was initiated in 1902, before any of the other great gardens, excepting La Mortola, were even contemplated – earlier even than Ellen Willmott's Boccanegra. It was the passion of one woman, spanning nearly three generations. Norah Warre, then Norah Bainbridge, was only eighteen when she first came to Roquebrune, and the garden was to remain hers until she died in her one hundredth year. She became the most knowledgeable plantswoman on the Riviera, to whom Wisley and Kew Gardens frequently sent plants to be tried and studied: she left it to the men – Lawrence ('Johnnie') Johnston, Charles de Noailles and Basil Leng – to bring back trophies from plant safaris. Twice widowed, and alone for the last thirty years of her life, she rather enjoyed the company and attention of Johnnie, Charles and Basil. Since her death, thanks to the intelligent and sensitive handling of the Roquebrune garden by her friends, it has emerged largely unscathed – an exceptional success story.

ABOVE: THIS PHOTOGRAPH WAS TAKEN BY PIPPA IRWIN AT VILLA ROQUEBRUNE TOWARDS THE END OF NORAH WARRE'S LIFE.

When Norah met the father of one of her school-friends, Emerson Bainbridge, it had been love at first sight. But at the first glimpse of her future home on a 'barren chaos of rock', she burst into tears. Until the villa was built, they lived in a prefabricated house which they had bought following a visit to the Paris Exposition of 1900 – it still stands in Roquebrune. The glory of Roquebrune was the view, which was painted by Monet, and which led Ernest de Ganay to nickname it *Balcon-sur-Mer*. In those days the landscape consisted of terraces of olive groves and citrus orchards running down to the sea. 'Oh my view,' Norah would lament as, across the Bay, the relentless rise and rise of Monte Carlo destroyed her picture postcard scene.

The terrain was similar to that of Boccanegra in many respects: exposed, south-facing, sheltered; sloping steeply to the sea, complete with railway running along the shore. It was a daunting site for any gardener. The rocks and boulders had to be beaten into terraces, water found, and every cubic inch of fertile red loam imported. Throughout Norah's seventy-five years there, finding suitable places for planting, with sufficient soil and space for roots, was always a problem.

The impetus for the garden came from her husband. He recruited a young gardener from Kew, who was there initially only to advise and help lay out the garden, but who stayed on. As it took shape and the emphasis switched to the plants rather than design, Norah's interest grew. She found she did not share the English fixation for green lawns; nor did she feel tempted to Italianize the garden. With the perennial problem of finding soil, there was no 'grand plan'. Instead it evolved as the plants arrived, and thus became a canopy of pines and exotic trees, with narrow, scampering paths, stone steps, and a luxuriance of planting completely masking the terraced design: a wonderland of differing dimensions. There were intimate corners and little clearings full of surprises, and tantalizing glimpses of the Mediterranean. She used many silver plants to brighten the undergrowth. 'The wind is your enemy,' she would say, 'so don't cut down too many pines.'

LEFT: NASTURTIUMS BRIGHTEN UP THE DARK AREAS UNDER THE ORANGE GROVE COMPLEMENTING THE BRIGHTLY COLOURED STRELITZIAS AND FERTILIZING THE SOIL BY THEIR NITROGEN CONTENT.

A PAIR OF MAGNIFICENT CYCAS
REVOLUTA AT VILLA
ROQUEBRUNE, APTLY DUBBED
'BALCON SUR MER'.

Just before the First World War, Bainbridge died. A few years later Norah married George, or 'Ginger', Warre, of the well-known port family. He too was a keen gardener, and raised the bearded iris *Tessa* at Roquebrune. Jim Russell, director of Sunningdale Nurseries, remembers going to stay at Roquebrune in 1938. 'It was a most luxurious villa with a marvellous collection of plants arranged with great taste. From the trees hung wicker cages full of exotic birds.' Basil Leng described them thirty years later as canaries of various shades of yellow. There was also a parakeet who bit people. After the Second World War, Ginger died in England.

Norah loved warmth but hated the fierce heat of summer. She much regretted her choice of iron, rather than wood, for the pergola, which frazzled the roses. Her summers were always spent in England, but even so she could not resist planting jacaranda, agapanthus or amaryllis, none of which she would ever see in flower. Kew, Wisley and several other institutions sent plants. She amassed a superb collection of jasmines and English and Nabonnand roses, which romped up trees and over walls. There were red and purple passion flowers, bignonias and strelitzias, arums, eucalyptus, yucca and euphorbias, and one part of the garden was devoted entirely to succulents. She particularly liked South African and Australian species, which she acclimatized so well that they did better than the indigenous cistus. Lawrence Johnston gave her many of his South African plants, as well as the famous *Jasminum polyanthum* which he and George Forrest brought back from their expedition to Yunnan. She adored red calliandras, mimosas and buddleias, especially the winter-flowering yellow *Buddleia madagascariensis*.

Although a welcoming hostess, Norah wasn't particularly keen on houseguests, and those who did come were expected to help in the garden – they were given a basket and sent off to weed. One was 'thought not to be much good if you were sunning yourself or reading a book,' said Pippa Irwin, a friend of her daughter, who fitted in because she devoted herself entirely to the garden, and performed the invaluable task of labelling all the plants. 'Norah was wonderful to be around,' she says, 'because of the thrill, the enthusiasm and curiosity, looking up plants in the "Bot Mag" to see if we were labelling them correctly.' Norah knew and respected Pippa's grandfather, the well-known botanist, Hiatt Baker. He too was a friend of Johnnie Johnston and Basil Leng, so there was an immediate *rapport*.

Another good friend was Renée Iliffe. When Norah was finally bedridden and nearly blind, she would ask Renée to bring her a flower from the garden. The instructions were given precisely and faultlessly. The flower would be brought in; she would feel it, and smell it, and yes, it was 'her'. 'Flowers were people to her,' Lady Iliffe recalls. 'Oh, she's doing rather badly,' Norah would say – referring to a plant, not a person. The charming and knowledgeable Charles de Noailles would arrive for lunch and enquire after 'Mrs Warre', referring not to his hostess but to the tree peony bred by Fred Stern of Highdown, which had gained a First Class Certificate from the RHS in 1953. 'A bad doer,' came the reply.

Norah Warre always said she hoped she would drop dead in her garden, but as she declined, her daughters brought her back to England, where she could be better cared for – and where she died. Her ashes, however, were scattered at Roquebrune, in the presence of her devoted staff and old friends who included Pippa Irwin and Renée Iliffe. It was decided not to sell the property to someone who might not look after it, so a preservation order was obtained. The *société* that bought the villa divided the interior into eight apartments, but left the outside unspoiled. 'They understood that the garden was rare and special, and became quite proud of it,' notes Lady Iliffe. She has ensured that the garden remains rare and special by bringing in Bruno Goris, a plantsman with impeccable taste. Bruno feels that the garden's remarkable beauty, apart from its dazzling collection of plants and trees, lies in the 'imbrication of the foliage' – the gliding together and overlapping of colours, forms and textures – and the repetition of good plants. Together they keep adding to the collection and making good the loss of plants that happened after her death. Another cause of plant loss has been automatic watering, which does not allow for individual plant requirements.

'A remarkable garden,' noted Edith Wharton in her diary, which seldom contained praise. 'She was a gallant gardener,' said Pippa Irwin of her great friend. For Norah Warre, who had gardened for seventy-five years on the 'barren chaos of rock' that became her passion, it seems a highly appropriate epitaph.

THESE STRELITZIAS, COMMONLY KNOWN AS BIRDS OF PARADISE, ARE A FEATURE OF MANY OF THE MORE SOPHISTICATED RIVIERA GARDENS.

Chapter Two
FRENCH PURISTS

———•———

. . . before 1914, Menton was practically an English dependence. Most of the hotels contained only English people. I remember that, in one of them where I was staying, a Frenchman took a room. He was looked at with astonishment, and referred to as 'the Frenchman'. An astonishing thought crossed my mind. There had been people here before the English. They had cultivated olives on a complex series of terraces, had lived in these steep streets of stone houses, perched high out of reach of pirates, and had thought nothing about sanitation. Needless to say my parents were not at all interested in these banal observations, but they mark a state in my consciousness.

SIR KENNETH CLARK

ASTUTELY PERCEIVED THROUGH THE EYES OF TEN-YEAR-OLD Kenneth Clark, the proprietorial attitude of the English eclipsed the French and their culture together – including a gardening tradition of *potager* (kitchen garden) and parterre, of *jardin à la française* and stunning botanical collections.

The French Renaissance gardens like the Jardin d'Albertas, or the gardens of the Château de Roussan, the parterres of the Châteaux of Beauregard, Entrecasteaux and Gourdon, each one attributed to Le Nôtre could have been equally at home adorning a château near Paris. In fact, it is said that the only authentic Le Nôtre garden was sketched at the close of a Paris soirée on the back of a dinner napkin for friends or cousins of Mme de Sévigné, who had bought the Château d'Entrecasteaux. These gardens were all derived from the French classical tradition, but bore no Mediterranean stamp. The Riviera, isolated from the rest of France by its singular climate and geography, looked for natural traditions, but could find nothing grander than a *potager* and a parcel of vines to call its own.

Most of the landscape was rock, distant white mountain peaks and wild scrub – the *maquis* by the sea, the *garrigue* inland – and where there was soil peasants had created terraces of olive groves, and citrus orchards: it was a classical landscape, a cultivated paradise. Guy de Maupassant dismissed it as a 'prettified watercolour decor furnished by a complaisant creator to inspire English gardeners'. These 'foreigners'

CHATEAU DE ROUSSAN, THE FORMER HOME OF THE NOSTRADAMUS FAMILY, IS NOW A HOTEL.

75

THIS SCENE AT CHATEAU DE ROUSSAN IN ST REMY IN PROVENCE COULD BE IN THE JARDIN DES PLANTES IN PARIS WERE IT NOT FOR A PALM TREE GROWING OUTSIDE. PICTURED HERE IS THE HARDIEST OF THE PALMS, CHAMAEROPS EXCELSA.

bought these olive groves and 'settled here,' protested Mérimée, 'as if in conquered territory'. They ripped out the *potagers*, dug up the parterres, vineyards and orchards, planting specimen trees and laying down lawns. They helped themselves to the range of exotic plants available in nurseries and from botanical gardens, and introduced a great number themselves, then they proceeded to make gardens in every style but French – for where was the thrill merely in repeating what was already there? The French purists reacted vehemently, pouring scorn on these fatuous lawns and elaborate Italian conceits as fast as the English poured out good money to pay for them. 'They deserve to be impaled upon the architecture which they have brought' rang the verdict of Mérimée, while Maupassant described the villas he saw from his yacht as 'white eggs laid during the night'. Pink palazzos such as Baroness Ephrussi de Rothschild's Ile de France were regarded as vulgar gin palaces.

Those tracts of wild scrub and rocks that the Parisian, the Russian, the English and the American had not yet over-cultivated were venerated by the purists like shrines. This colonized *terroir* had to find its own identity, a vernacular, an idiom all of its own; and it *was* found: not by the botanists or the plantsmen, but by designers such as Ferdinand Bac and Coco Chanel, who looked no further for their inspiration than the shores of the Mediterranean and the wild plants that grew along it. When Chanel bought La Pausa in 1928, the first thing she did was demolish the villa and replant the garden.

RIGHT: FERDINAND BAC'S GREAT LOVE WAS CYPRESSES; THESE PLANTED BY HIM AND NOW GROWN TALL MIRROR THE STEEPLES OF OLD MENTON.

COCO CHANEL WAS AS
INNOVATIVE WITH HER
GARDEN AS SHE WAS WITH
HER CLOTHES.

The landscape designer Ferdinand Bac wanted to do away with what he called the 'cosmopolitan profanity of the Côte d'Azur' and re-establish a Mediterranean style – the problem being that no such style existed. The garden he designed in Menton for the Laden Bockairys – with whom he would live, die and even be buried – was called Les Colombières. It was a nostalgic architectural evocation of all his travels in Spain, Italy and Greece; it was classical, it was Latin, but it was not local. The olive, the carob, the cypress were his gods, and all architectural features were erected in homage to them: a staircase built around a thousand-year-old carob tree, a cypress used as a focal point. Views were framed and brought into the garden like pictures placed on a wall.

Chanel first saw La Pausa two years after her friend Colette bought La Treille Muscate in 1925. La Pausa, said Visconti, was Chanel's 'place of beauty, serenity and comfort'. It also symbolized her hopes of marriage with Bendor, Duke of Westminster – and then her dashed dreams. It was set high above Roquebrune with spectacular views to the sea; the drive led through olive groves and mimosa and jacaranda to a 'new' Roman villa designed by architect Robert Streitz. It had a vaulted entrance and an inner courtyard enclosed by grey-white stucco walls and tiled roof. She furnished the interior with unfashionable Provençal and Spanish pieces and, with help from her 'no-colour sisters' Lady Mendl and Syrie Maugham, decorated it in browns, beiges and white, with leather and chamois sofas. Every room was filled with vases of tuberoses and lavenders. Rory Cameron referred to the atmospheric quality of her garden, planted only with lavender and rosemary, and the subtle effect of smoky light filtering through the olives. 'Her gardens were special again. She was the first to cultivate "poor" plants like lavender and olive trees, and discard lilies, roses and flowers of that kind.'

Chanel and Colette used to tear around the Riviera in Chanel's Rolls Royce, exploring the coast and the *arrière-pays*, scouting for artisans in the hilltop villages. They had both escaped their provincial upbringing and made a success of themselves in a practical and unassuming way; their Riviera homes expressing their singular personality. In 1950 La Pausa was bought by Churchill's literary agent Emery Reves, whose American wife Wendy covered the whole garden in a sea of lavender.

The exotic and anti-exotic wars, and the disagreement over the use of colour in a garden remain intellectual arguments – the eucalyptus, the palm tree and that other sub-tropical, the mimosa, have now integrated themselves so well into the landscape as to appear native – and even the ancient cypress worshipped by Bac was not really native, but imported from Greece and Persia in the sixteenth century. There is no such argument, however, about the *potager*: it came with the Ark. A necessity rather than an aesthetic pleasure, it is an art form nevertheless.

In nearby Biot there lives a basket weaver who could easily have been numbered amongst Renoir's friends – or indeed, have been the very Italian, Canova, who tended the Renoir *potager* at Les Collettes and sang Piedmontese choruses under the olive trees. Almost a century

later, René Ghiglione can be found on the tiny terrace of his own *potager* on a Saturday evening, singing with up to twenty of his friends. In this garden, which is more sophisticated than all the stylistic fabrications of the garden wizards, the rituals and traditions go back to much earlier cultures.

Today, the calm countenance of the bearded master basket weaver of Biot reveals his philosophy of living. The grandson of a charcoal burner, René had an almost mythical childhood in the cork oak and sweet chestnut-clad forests of les Maures. He would accompany the elders of the village of Mayons on their walks into the forest to tend gardens composed around a little spring, or grotto. In clearings in the forest planted with vegetables, he would listen to their tales of forest hermits, legends going back many centuries, and learn about thousand-year-old pagan traditions broken by modern culture and society – a culture based on profitability, where time is money; a society which thinks itself superior to Nature. In Nature, he argues, there is no anarchy. Living for a time in a forest clearing beside the river, he raised goats, grew vegetables, and learned the craft of his father, who was a shepherd before becoming a basket weaver. Now a father himself, René gardens organically. He also raises goats for milk and rabbits for meat. They are killed swiftly – not 'with gaiety in my heart, but with a little prayer beforehand' – and their blood is spilled on the base of the plants. This little garden, which he calls a *'jardin d'accomplissement'*, where he attempts *'de bien rêver ma vie'*, is his life's work, his karma.

THE TERRACE OF RENE GHIGLIONE'S LITTLE CABANON BY HIS POTAGER IS PERFECT IN EVERY DETAIL.

LEFT: RENE'S ORGANIC
POTAGER FEATURES CHARD
AND COMPANION PLANTS.

Here he tries to enact the essential values of life: respect for others, and for the order of Nature.

An interesting link exists between René and La Pausa. The house that Coco Chanel bought is called La Pausa because it stands on the spot where Mary Magdalene was believed to have rested during her flight from Jerusalem; and the grotto in the forest where René goes for meditation is where she is said to have made her permanent home.

La Louve

NICOLE DE VESIAN

Step through the front door of La Louve and in an instant you have the essence of the Lubéron in what feels like a rather exotic quarry. The rough walls have been chiselled from golden rock; the pervasive smell of lavender fills the air; and under your feet lies a floor of loose, smooth stones.

Indifferent to the acquisitive pursuits of a plantsman or the introduction of exotica; completely uninterested, in fact, in growing flowers, this is a purist's garden; a sober architectural world of hewn rock, of

BELOW: THE STRIKINGLY
MODERN GARRIGUE STYLE OF
NICOLE DE VESIAN'S GARDEN
IN PROVENCE.

sculpted greens and greys, a textured tableau of aromatics and stones, or of plants that can be made to look like stones; a stylized distillation of the Lubéron landscape, where shape and volume are fashioned by the hand that wields the secateurs and garden shears. Box and yew have been released from the rank and file of the parterre, and rosemary, santolina, myrtle and lonicera plucked from the anonymity of the *garrigue*, clipped into mounds, and made to look distinctive. It is a garden which hugs the earth: the work of a man, one would think, perhaps an architect or a sculptor. But occasional incongruities appear: a purple allium, a few orange gaillardias, a scarlet hybrid tea. It is said that when you garden like a man you are ruthless with your plants, but here those plants that seed themselves, or are gifts from friends, are allowed to stay.

Both house and garden have been devised as a practical and aesthetic response to the challenges and requirements of Nicole de Vésian's life, always with wit and flair – because otherwise, as she says, why do it at all? Nicole's father was a Welsh banker; her mother came from Avignon. She was brought up in Paris by an English nanny with her three extremely handsome, capable and much admired brothers. 'Pity about the girl,' people would say, looking at the four of them; 'I like the boys but I don't like the girl,' Nanny's voice rang every morning. 'I was an idiot,' says Nicole, *'une cruche*. I achieved nothing. I went to school in Paris and was married off at seventeen.' She led the life of a Parisian housewife until 1939 when the war changed everything. She took her two children to Aix-les-Bains, and had to make do with nothing. She fashioned the children's clothes from old curtains, bred rabbits for fur to make coats, cut up her Hermès handbags to repair the soles of shoes, planted beetroot to make jam. Gertrude Stein nearly ran her over on her bicycle and offered to give her English lessons. Nicole remembers Alice B. Toklas in a big black hat, endlessly cooking, and Gertrude Stein, standing in the middle of the kitchen, always barefoot, wearing

sackcloth. 'The war taught me to fight, that nothing was impossible – you just get up and do it. I was rather sad when normal life returned. It was a time when one had value according to what one could do. I think that's how I continue to operate now. If I want something I'll think of a way to do it, and although it may not turn out exactly right, it might lead to something else, to another point of view. I think I've applied this to the garden.'

Her present garden style stems from a former home in Port Grimaud, a clever pastiche of Venice and one of very few architecturally successful large-scale 'developments' on the Riviera. When she bought the house in Port Grimaud, lured south *par choix de soleil*, she was raising five children with the help of a *demoiselle* and had started her own marketing consultancy firm in Paris to support both her family and a chronically unwell husband. Time was of the essence – and so was money. 'We had to fight to get things, or invent them and given them punch.' The pressures of a family, an office and travel all weighed upon her, and working in a chic social milieu, you had to look the part. She knew

NICOLE DE VESIAN SEATED NEXT TO SELF-SEEDING HOLLYHOCKS.

that with a wardrobe of grey, beige and black, one couldn't go wrong –
and a string of pearls in the glove compartment added instant chic.
Even now people look at her trousers and say: Hermès? No, the flea
market at Apt; but maybe an Hermès belt is added once in a while for a
little bit of glory. Nicole operated her business from a basement flat
within the Elysée Palace compound, her staff all women, and in her
many years there never once locked her office door. Frequent trips to
Milan meant that a little place in Port Grimaud would be a pied à terre
to which she could escape, even if it was only for one night. The house
was right on the beach and she immediately started planting to make it
attractive. Rising at six, she went to the mountains to collect stones and
dig up cistus, rosemary, juniper and lavender. 'It was a struggle to get
things to grow, so I learned to grow things that wanted to grow, and
every time I left, I cut back the lavenders and the rosemaries *à mort.*'
She protected their roots with stones against the scorching sun, the
wind and seaspray, so on her return she found the garden more or less
as she had left it. 'That is what gave me the taste for pruning and clipping.' It was simple, it looked good, and it suited Nicole's character and
lifestyle. But as Port Grimaud became more fashionable and more
crowded, and the children no longer wanted to come, she began visiting
her cousins in Aix.

In this way she discovered the Lubéron. Attracted and intrigued by
its wildness she explored the region, one day discovering an old chapel
with a tiny garden in Bonnieux – and bought it almost as a lark. '*Je me*

THE SOFT YELLOW ACHILLEA,
DISTINCTIVE FOLIAGE OF THE
LOQUAT TREE AND STONE
URNS ARE REMINISCENT OF A
MEDIEVAL TAPESTRY.

suis prise au jeu.' Everyone said I was crazy.' Finding that plants seemed to grow easily, she filled her garden with red oleanders and geraniums. Then one day it seemed out of place, incongruous. 'I've created *un jardin de blanchisseuse*, it's so clumsy, so showy. So I gave the plants away and started again.' The hard winter of 1985 helped – by finishing the rest off. 'I always think we are too encumbered in life, and my way of coping has always been to simplify. When I came home I wanted calm. It shocks people I have no flowers in my garden, nothing on the walls either. I've got my paintings through the windows. I don't need the paintings and chintzes of others. At the beginning I shocked the nurserymen by wanting beige oleanders and beige roses and geraniums. They'd ring each other up to say "Have you seen this *folle* who's looking for beige plants?"'

When Nicole first saw La Louve, in the same village as her converted chapel, it had lain an abandoned ruin for many years. The garden was much larger and at first it was the stones which fascinated her and she just wanted to buy the garden and the stones. 'There was a lot of box, so I thought there must be water. The vendor said there wasn't. There must be a *bassin*? You're dreaming of castles, he said.' But Nicole came back one night with rubber gloves, secateurs and a lamp. She was certain there was a well somewhere and, scratching around in the dark, she found it.

Before buying La Louve, she asked if she could get to know the garden for a summer, and began by treating everything that was treatable: the few plants that were already there. 'It allowed me to *vivre le jardin*. I cut, pruned, clipped, fed, watered and had good results, but didn't really know where I was going.' One has a tendency to plan gardens standing up, but it's when you're sitting down that you look at it most. She made windows in the foliage to frame the views. She bought it by doing designing stints for Hermès – perhaps styling the inside of Jane Birkin's car, or a private aircraft. People say you can't start a garden after the age of forty. Nicole had been seventy. She would return each time from her apartment in Paris with a fresh eye, so the garden came together bit by bit.

José, a French-speaking Spanish mason, helped enormously. 'To simple people,' she says, 'nothing seems impossible. Only more sophisticated people always think of problems.' She had a call one day from his wife. 'Please calm José down,' she pleaded. 'He came back from your house so excited he started trimming the cypresses into balls.' On an errand one morning, Nicole slipped outside the Mairie and broke her leg. She left the hospital a year later – a year of working on medieval tapestries – and on her return home immediately planted two loquats.

Seasonal plants are dismissed. 'I don't like to see flowers and then afterwards, nothing.' The garden is filled with stones, trees and plants collected from the surrounding hills by Nicole herself. 'I don't want to have too tight a rein on the garden', she says. 'Graphic and balanced certainly, but a bit mad as well.' Some lavenders she crops tightly, while others, as a counterpoint, she leaves shaggy. Her beloved stones are placed all over the garden, but never fixed, because she might suddenly want to change them. As original as Nicole herself is this garden of moveable stones and steadfast plants.

NICOLE DE VESIAN'S GARDEN FEATURES STRONG LINES AND ARCHITECTURAL PLANTS.

THE VIEW FROM UNDER A
MUCH-LOVED LIME TREE ON
THE ESPLANADE AT THE
CHATEAU DU VIGNAL. THE
BORDER OF MEDITERRANEAN
PLANTS IS DOMINATED BY
GREY AND BLUE WITH A TINY
BIT OF ROSE.

CHATEAU DU VIGNAL

PIERO AND HENRIETTE CHIESA

The Château du Vignal differs from all the other gardens featured in this book in that it is the only one established by a truly local family who had lived in Nice long before it became a part of France in 1860. The Vignal was originally bought to escape from, rather than to embrace the summer heat, and was never intended to be a plantsman's garden, or a showpiece. It has basically remained the agricultural property it always was, with the garden evolving around a respect for the *terroir*. The towering surreal cypresses, the broad sweeps of the landscaped garden, the eclectic architecture, and the *bassins* are all on a grand scale – but are also *to* scale, a triumph of proportion. It is a very exciting place to be. The Gautier imagination has amused itself with the château and the simple lines of the garden; the restraint, the simplicity of the planting, and subtlety of colour all work, but do not compete with the château which, together with the light and space, provides the fireworks.

The bold lines of this panoramic garden, one of only three which can still claim to have inherited an unspoiled natural landscape, were carved out during the eras of Piero Chiesa's great-grandfather and grandfather, between 1860 and 1920. When the first Monsieur Gautier bought the château it was entirely surrounded by plane trees and a chestnut forest, with olive groves, an olive mill, and vineyards. Several styles of architecture have been added to the eleventh century tower, all of which have left their signature on the castle. The remarkable avenue of cypresses was copied from the villa of a relative near Florence. Albert Gautier Vignal, Piero's grandfather, developed the agricultural aspect by planting many more olives and, across the road, a vineyard that produced red and white wine.

When Albert died in 1939, he left the estate to his son, Louis, Piero's uncle. During the war the château was occupied by French, Italian and American troops, and when they left, the house remained closed. The family would return for picnics under the trees and Somerset Maugham often came up from Cap Ferrat to write in peace on the big stone table near the chapel. In 1970 Piero inherited the Vignal. He and Henriette found that the old chestnuts and laurels had seeded themselves in a dense thicket all around the castle. Pushing open the heavy walnut door, which had been locked for twenty-six years, they found the interior exactly as the troops had left it.

The family decided to undertake the intimidating task of restoring both the château and the gardens with the help and advice of their friends Pierre and Nicole Champin of the Chèvre d'Or. For the Gautier family, Le Vignal had always been 'the carnation in the buttonhole', but on a limited budget and based in Milan, the Chiesas had to do it all themselves during the weekends and holidays. Like Humphrey Waterfield and his 'one *bassin* a year' Water Staircase, the château became a

AN IMPRESSIVE BANK OF HYDRANGEA QUERCIFOLIA LEADS TO THE PORTE DE NARBONNE – A PILGRIM'S RESTING PLACE.

'two rooms a year' project; and gradually, through enthusiasm, imagination and an enormous amount of hard work, the château was sublimely restored and furnished.

At the same time, they continued to remove the trees overshadowing the château, drawing cries of protest from the children. 'You're turning it into a desert!' Thinning the jungle involved difficult planning decisions and a great deal of soul searching. But the house and courtyards had been so cloaked in darkness that drastic action was called for. Letting in more light allowed peonies and lilies to awake once more. Then, in 1986, the great fires which devastated thousands of acres across the *arrière-pays* of Nice, swept through the top half of the estate. It was Henriette's birthday, and she was all alone in the house. As a surprise, however, Piero arrived from Milan. He found fires raging all around, and that the neighbours had come to take refuge at the château – 'So in the end we were quite numerous, but we had very little water. You can do quite a lot with pails and brooms.' Fortunately, the estate is bisected by a road, which acted as a fire break, and by a miracle the château and gardens were untouched.

Piero and Henriette wanted a garden that was airy and ordered, that smelt good, would be easy to maintain and would also harmonize with the landscape. For this they looked to the subtle beauty of the indigenous, Mediterranean plants. Guido Piacenza was consulted and he supplied a collection of rosemaries, cistuses, lavender, santolinas and old roses with which to begin the transition. On the sound principle that it is more economical to grow one crop than several, the vines were pulled up and replaced with olives, in order to concentrate on the production of oil. Seven hundred olive trees now produce several hundred litres of oil, which, pressed in their ancient local olive mill, has been awarded Premier Prix. As with wine, the quality of oil is always dependent on the vagaries of climate. Henriette, herself a descendent of a noted botanist, runs a small but well-known vineyard in Switzerland producing Vinzel wine. Curiously, both the ownership and the care of the vines have passed from mother to daughter for five generations. Five generations of women *vigneronnes* have grown, harvested and pressed the grapes, and the sixth generation are daughters too. Henriette and Piero divided their time between these two estates and their home in Milan, where they live '*délicieusement*', overlooking the old botanical garden. Life in Milan creates '*un désir de nature*', she says, 'and you get to a certain age where you start becoming more interested in the garden but unfortunately you don't always have the energy you once had to go with it! Let the Good Lord send us somebody,' they said to Jane Harvey, who is currently restoring Villa Noailles. She sent them Bruno Goris. On his advice, the Chiesas are adding to their collection of purely Mediterranean plants, and to the many roses already planted by Edith Gautier over fifty years ago, including Alberic Barbier scrambling up a cypress. 'The garden,' says Bruno, 'has a personality, and I'm not going to change it.'

SEEN FROM THE ROOF OF THE CHATEAU, THIS TOWERING CYPRESS GIVES AN IDEA OF THE SCALE AND PROPORTION OF THE GARDEN.

Chapter Three
STYLE BARONS

———— • ————

HAROLD PETO, LAWRENCE 'JOHNNIE' JOHNSTON, EDITH Wharton and Charles de Noailles were the creative nucleus whose aesthetic sensibility and plantmanship would profoundly shape the style and content of Riviera gardens. The influence spanned nearly the whole century, starting with the revival on both sides of the Atlantic of the Italian Renaissance garden; in America with the publication of Edith Wharton's classic book *Italian Villas and Their Gardens* in 1904, and in England with the work of architect Harold Peto.

When Peto left his architectural partnership with Ernest George to concentrate on gardens, the stipulation that he was not to work in England for fifteen years took him to the Riviera. Had he stayed in England, he might well have created the style of garden that made Hidcote famous. Victorian bedding and Capability Brown parkland was definitely old hat and a new idiom began to emerge, recalled from the Jacobean garden of hedges, topiary and rose, with cottage garden planting. When Lawrence Johnston began creating the gardens at Hidcote in 1907, he had read Wharton's book, which spoke of garden compartments and colour themes; harmony between house and garden, garden and landscape. These were the ideas he would apply to Hidcote with his now famous yew hedges and red border, and which Wharton was busily realizing at her home The Mount, in Lenox, Massachusetts. She had a 'red garden' already in place in 1905. There was also another link. Wharton was a friend of Lady Elcho from Stanway, the doyenne of the All Souls – a circle of enlightened and artistic aristocrats to which Norah Lindsay also belonged. Both she and Lawrence Johnston developed the 'jungle of beauty' effect which has dominated certain English gardens ever since.

The principles of classic garden design found their way into many places, but nowhere more appropriately than on the Riviera, where the climate, the landscape, the 'terracing' and magic black sentinel cypress already had an Italian character – indeed it was a region that had once belonged to Italy. By 1910 Harold Peto had exploited this to the full, having created three Italian dreamlands on Cap Ferrat: Villa Sylvia, Villa Maryland and Villa Rosemary – every brush-stroke his own, from the architect's drawings down to the last spoon. One could say that his

CHARLES DE NOAILLES' GARDEN IS FILLED WITH ORNAMENTS SUCH AS THIS FAUN PLAYING A FLUTE. THE CIRCULAR BASSIN COMES FROM AN ANCIENT OLIVE MILL.

passion for Italy was derivative, but his personal genius lay in his inventive, dazzling use of colour, which everyone flocked to study and admire, including Edith Wharton, Lawrence Johnston, and Cecil and Dorothy Hanbury. Returning from a visit in March 1922, Wharton reported to her niece Beatrix Farrand, the American landscape designer: 'Absolutely dazzling – *pure flower gardening* . . . sheets of radiant colour.'

In the early 1920s, Edith Wharton was living permanently in Paris. While holidaying in Hyères, she accidentally stumbled upon Castel Ste Claire, an abandoned convent. She fell in love and leased it. Soon after, Johnnie Johnston bought Serre de la Madone in Menton, to be near to his mother who was in the sanatorium there. The trio was completed by the arrival of the newly married thirty-two-year-old Vicomte Charles de Noailles, whose mother had bought him the land next to Ste Claire at the suggestion of her friend Edith Wharton. It was called Parc St Bernard. These three 'aristocrats of the spirit', who became the 'unofficial' French branch of the All Souls, had previously all known each other in England. While at Cambridge, the nineteen-year-old Charles had served as a plant courier for rhododendron seeds which Johnston was sending to his friend Guillaume Mallet at Bois des Moutiers, the Lutyens-Jekyll house near Dieppe.

A path connected the two Saints, Bernard and Claire – and would be well trodden for the next fifteen years. It was a mutual interest in gardening which sparked off the friendship between Charles, an enthusiastic but inexperienced young gardener, and his neighbour, Edith, the experienced teacher, and thirty years his senior.

Each household had its own circle of artistic and literary friends, the Paris 'salon' society having moved en masse to the Riviera, where there was good food, good conversation, and many picnics and walks in the hills. The Ste Claire entourage included Johnston, Kenneth and Jane Clark, Bernard and Mary Berenson, Nicky Mariano, Aldous and Maria Huxley, and Cyril and Jean Connolly. Huxley admitted that Edith Wharton's short novel *Twilight Sleep* had influenced *Brave New World*, and it may have been she who spurred him out into the garden. Maria reported Aldous digging 'every spare inch of the ground and causing havoc all around him to the despair of the gardener'.

The young Noailles couple, who had built a strikingly modern cubist style house within the ramparts of the ruined castle at St Bernard, were wealthy patrons of then unknown avant-garde artists and composers such as Poulenc, Man Ray and Jean Cocteau. Sometimes the socializing between the two camps went well; sometimes it was disastrous. At the Noailles' home, one afternoon, Cocteau, wanting to expose and ridicule Bernard Berenson's hatred of modern art, played a joke on him. Pointing to his own concoction on canvas of a black circle, newsprint and sackcloth, he said it was by Picasso, and as good as anything by Berenson's beloved Raphael. A heated argument ensued, from which Berenson came away very distraught, but no one in the Wharton set was ever told that it had been a hoax to embarrass Berenson.

EDITH WHARTON WITH HER TWO PEKES AND HER HOUSEKEEPER CATHERINE GROSS ON THE TERRACE OF STE CLAIRE LE CHATEAU.

It was not only an artistic and literary colony that sprang up, but also a gardening club. Johnnie Johnston and later Basil Leng appeared on the scene and they all swapped plants, talked plants, dipped in and out of their favourite gardens and nurseries; and the 'boys' all went plant hunting together. A constant stream of guests made their way between the two houses like a column of ants for tea, lunch and dinner from December to March for the next fifteen years.

Edith and Johnnie had swapped their famous green and reasonably flat 'garden rooms' for 'terrace' rooms which descended quite dramatically. Now they were working with a garden in a different dimension, and within each terrace could experiment with themes and colours. Edith was ten years older than Johnnie, but they shared an American background, which neither of them cared for much, and a European sensibility which they thrived on. Both felt at home among the old civilizations which loved beauty, peace and the arts – the very things that were being swallowed up in America by Fords and cinemas. Edith admired Johnnie's gardens tremendously – she 'revelled' in his garden at Menton; Hidcote she found 'tormentingly perfect', and called it a 'green peace of a garden, different from the one at Menton but equally perfect'. At 'Madame', her nickname for Serre de la Madone, she mooned over a pale lemon datura – 'that was covered with flowers growing next to a lemon tree covered with fruit, and you cannot imagine anything more beautiful', as she wrote to her niece Beatrix Farrand.

THE CUBIST GARDEN AT VILLA NOAILLES IN HYERES FORMERLY HAD A BRANCUSI STATUE AT THE END, BUT IT WAS STOLEN. PLANTING CHANGES EVERY YEAR: THE BLUE AND YELLOW PANSIES HAVE NOW BEEN REPLACED BY WALLFLOWERS AND STOCKS.

The first of many Riviera encounters between Edith and Johnnie Johnston was recorded in her diary on 23 March 1923, when Lady Colefax (who would later persuade him to hand Hidcote to the National Trust) brought him to lunch. The following year he arrived as a houseguest and set a pattern that prevailed until her death. They would walk around the garden together and for three days visit various gardens, nurseries and friends. They went to La Mortola, where they had tea with the Hanburys, once sharing a picnic lunch in the head gardener's house; and the Hanburys would return the call, bringing the Duke of Connaught with them. They often went to the Jardin de Plantes Grasses, in Monte Carlo, for cacti and succulents; to Lord Brougham's Villa Eléonore, in Cannes, for the roses; to Entrecasteaux, and the Château de Gourdon for a pleasant day out. They also went to Norah Warre's garden, to look, without a doubt, at the formidable array of plants – which Edith, in another rare complimentary notation, found 'remarkable'. She even went plant hunting with Johnnie in April of 1931, looking for *Iris olbiensis* in the *arrière-pays*.

Their favourite nurseries were the Crovettos' in Menton, Ruby's in Cannes, and that of Monsieur Denis, the iris grower at Tamaris, another favourite haunt. Roses and camellias came from the Schneider sisters in Cannes but the absolute favourite nurserymen were the Jahandiez brothers in Carquierrane, who were former gardeners to the Rothschilds. They specialized in succulents and are mentioned so many times in Wharton's diary that their nursery could have been a second home. An engaging picture of Emile Jahandiez is provided by 'Cherry' Ingram, who, while searching for *Prunus prostrata*, the rock cherry, came across a rather extraordinary fellow in shabby clothes and carpet slippers. 'That he was a professional botanist was plain to see for he had a very old and very battered vasculum slung over his left shoulder . . . It did not take me long to realize that I was talking to someone who possessed a knowledge of the local flora that was second to none.'

Johnnie sometimes sent his gardener to Ste Claire, and Edith would take him to see Jahandiez. By 1926 Basil Leng, 'the most knowledgeable gardener on the coast' according to Edith, had arrived on the scene. In 1932 he brought with him to Ste Claire 'a very pretty Madame Pierre Champin'. Her garden, La Chèvre d'Or in Biot, created with her husband Pierre, became one of the first gardens to be planted outside the winter months. They were greatly helped by Basil Leng's knowledge of plants. Each year Edith and Charles 'motored to see the cherry blossom' together, and then

STE CLAIRE LE CHATEAU AT HYERES, AN ABANDONED CONVENT WITHIN MEDIEVAL CASTLE WALLS, WAS THE WINTER HOME OF EDITH WHARTON UNTIL HER DEATH IN 1937.

in 1937, on what would be her last birthday, she noted that 'Charles kept everyone laughing' at Ste Claire. It is curious, though, that she never mentions or passes comment on his garden. However, he called her 'a great gardener, and very serious technically'.

After Edith Wharton's death in 1937 Johnnie and Charles remained friends. They continued to play tennis and squash together, and were in the process of organizing a plant-hunting expedition to Burma when the outbreak of the war put an end to their plans. Johnnie's planthunting days were over, but Charles de Noailles went on distributing plants to gardeners all over the Riviera until his death in 1981.

SERRE DE LA MADONE

MAJOR LAWRENCE JOHNSTON

A SHADY BASSIN AT SERRE DE
LA MADONE.

The enigmatic Major Lawrence Johnston has kept people guessing for
years. His garden is the most renowned of modern English gardens, as
visited and talked about as Vita Sackville-West's Sissinghurst – but
whereas she poured her heart out daily, he never seemed to speak or
write. The first thing that anyone says about him is that he had a bossy
mother.

'Johnnie' Johnston has been described as a 'small man with fair hair
and very blue eyes, shy, modest and scrupulous'. He hated publicity,
never gave any interviews, and his letters seemed to consist mostly of
plant lists. The only clue to a livelier side to him comes from Edith's
diary, which unusually records 'a jolly conversation with Johnnie'. He
painted, and collected tiles, lead watering cans, iron seats and Anduze
jars. He was also a devout Catholic and had a small chapel built at Hidcote. He was not at all sociable – even Maybud Campbell, the Queen of
Menton, who knew of his garden, didn't know what he looked like until
he was pointed out to her at a tennis club – but had a wide circle of gardening friends and cultivated most of the leading nurserymen in
France. He is often called a 'Howard Sturges' American, one born in
America but spending less than ten of his eighty-seven years there. His
mother, Gertrude Johnston, must have considered herself French,
because the staff at Hidcote always called her Madame.

He was born in 1871 in Paris to wealthy East Coast American parents, but did not live in New York until he was nearly ten. By this time his younger brother and sister had both died, and three years later his father was also dead. This may help to explain the possessive nature of his mother, who subsequently also lost her second husband after eleven years of marriage. 'I can see her now,' James Lees-Milne remarked recently, 'swathed in purple from goitre to ankle'.

Johnnie Johnston read History at Cambridge University, became a naturalized British citizen, joined the army and fought for a year in the Boer War in South Africa, where he would later go plant hunting. His mother bought Hidcote, a three-hundred-year-old Cotswold farm, for the two of them in 1907, and he farmed and gardened there until he went to war in 1914. Two years into the war, he was badly wounded and left among the dead awaiting burial. Miraculously, however, he was recognized by a Cotswold neighbour, who also saw him twitch. Invalided out of the army, he returned to Hidcote with a badly damaged lung. Six years later his mother began suffering from senile dementia. On the recommendation of the influential Doctor Bennet they sought relief from the English winter in Menton, and in the early 1920s began looking for a villa near to Gertrude Johnston's sanatorium at Gorbio, above Menton. They bought Serre de la Madone in 1924, and she died there two years later.

Ernest de Ganay, who described Johnston as a 'gentleman gardener', a hunter of plants, recalls visiting Serre de la Madone, where

Johnston came out to greet him dressed in velvet corduroy, with earth-stained hands. Charles de Noailles quoted Johnnie Johnston flippantly remarking that he had never bought a plant – 'All my plants were either given to me by friends or picked up along the roadside.' He did buy plants, of course, but the swapping of plants was not only a courtesy, it was a necessity. And he chose particularly those gardens where he thought his plants would do better than in his own. That way, if something he had collected on a roadside somewhere died, he would know where to find it again. These casual 'roadsides' he was referring to just happened to be in South Africa, Mexico and Yunnan, China, where he went plant hunting, bringing back for La Serre plants which he had no hope of growing out of doors at Hidcote. In fact, a part of the garden was simply known as Mexico.

In 1927, the year after his mother died, he went to South Africa for three months with Cherry Ingram and Sir George Ingram. Jim Russell remembers Cherry Ingram talking about it. They had three lorries, one to travel in, one fitted up as a sort of sitting-room and one for supplies and bedding. It was certainly a rather luxurious safari as Johnston's Italian cook and chauffeur–butler were brought along too! Described by Ingram as 'a typical bachelor completely dedicated to gardening', Johnston collected any genus he thought beautiful and sent most of it to the Royal Botanic Garden of Edinburgh and to his garden in Menton.

NATURE CREEPS STEALTHILY TOWARDS THE BOTTOM OF THE GARDEN. ONLY THE OUTLINE OF THE TERRACE REMAINS.

CHAPTER THREE

In 1931 he went with George Forrest on his last expedition to Yunnan in China. He brought back *Jasminum polyanthum*, and gave a piece
of it to his good friend Norah Warre. She sent it to England, where it
appeared in a botanical magazine, and every gardener in England
wanted it that year. He also collected *Mahonia siamensis* and *Mahonia
lomariifolia*. The former is tender, but grew very well in Menton, where
just before his death in 1958 it was still looking superb.

The terraced garden, with its old olive and citrus trees, sloped west-
ward, and was sheltered from every wind, enabling Johnston to grow
sub-tropical plants. It was a garden of pools, terraces and vistas, flights
of stone steps, broken by landings with little pools – an Italian feature –
and a rotunda with tightly pruned wisteria from which to take in the
whole garden.

This huge, peaceful garden must have seemed very tropical and
exotic, entirely surrounded by forest and inhabited by many birds, all
calling out to one another. They lived inside the ruined archways of an
enormous aviary which enclosed a section of the forest – among them
were a macaw, crowned and demoiselle cranes, ibis, flamingos, peacocks, golden and silver pheasants and a particularly nasty ancient
parrot. Cascading water, papyrus eight feet tall, and lotus blossom all
heightened the exotic effect; the sword leaves and scarlet flowers of the
Mexican beschorneria overhung a wall below which lay sheets of agapanthus.

The plants which Johnnie had collected from all over the world were
arranged with 'a wonderful architectural sense and an amazing eye for
colour'. With towering specimens of *Magnolia delavayi*, the Chilean
podocarpus, caesalpinia, enormous blue irises called *Lawrence Johnston*,
and red Persian tulips, the garden was a paradise of colours and per-
fumes sheltered by the mountains. The tropical effect was further
enhanced by night-flowering cactus cereus and strelitzias grown near
the house, and on the walls the fragrant evergreen trachelospermum
and *Hibiscus rosa-sinensis* growing amongst *Thunbergia grandiflora*.

On the terraces, which succeeded each other like 'open air rooms',
each with a different theme, were melaleucas, banksias, Chinese tree
peonies and California ceanothus. Each terrace was underplanted with
east Mediterranean tulips and South African bulbs; the paths were
edged with Algerian irises. Creeping plumbago and pink belladonna
lilies covered a nearby slope. Other striking features included a parterre of box, with a plane tree growing in the middle of each quarter,
and lined with double periwinkle through which thousands of cherry
and white striped Lady tulips grew. Japonica and reticulata camellias
also had a corner to themselves with lime-free soil. This list of plants
sent to the Cambridge University Botanic Garden after his death is
staggering; unfortunately, few have survived.

Johnston went on extending his garden, buying parcels of land from
nine different people until his ten hectares were completed in 1939.
Soon, however, he was being evacuated, when the Germans invaded
France in 1940, on the coal boat immortalized by Maugham. To be
truthful, he minded leaving his seven dogs behind far more than the
villa or his plants. Returning in 1943, he found that it had been occupied by the Italians, and was in the same mess that they left La Garoupe
and Vignal in. Soon afterwards he began suffering from senile dementia,

THE CAMELLIA CORNER
PLANTED WITH ACIDIC SOIL
SPECIALLY BROUGHT IN BY
THE TRAINLOAD BY THE
VICOMTE DE NOAILLES.

THE MADONE WELCOMES
VISITORS TO THE GARDEN, A
CURIOUS MIXTURE OF SUB-
TROPICAL PLANTS, WEEDS AND
RENAISSANCE MOTIFS.

as his mother had. It was around this time that Jim Russell, the director of Sunningdale Nurseries and later of the arboretum at Castle
Howard, first met him. 'His mind would flicker on and off and he could
seldom remember anything for any length of time. He was a most
charming and gentle person, and still remembered and cherished his
plants very much indeed.' After he died in 1958, La Serre was left to
Nancy Lindsay, Norah's daughter, but she could not afford to maintain
it, and it was broken up and its plants, birds and ornaments dispersed
among the Menton gardening fraternity. Jim Russell regrets the loss of
Johnston's French garden, which in many ways had a far more interesting collection of plants than Hidcote. La Serre is now only a
shadow of its former self, its exotic quality replaced by the haunting
stillness of a rather magical world gone quietly to sleep, and the Major
seems to have eluded us forever.

STE CLAIRE LE CHATEAU
EDITH WHARTON

Edith Wharton was born in New York but spent a large part of her childhood in Europe, making numerous trips to Italy, France and England. 'Papa,' she would ask her father after returning from each trip 'when are we going back again?'

On their last trip to Europe as a family, when Edith was nineteen, they went to Cannes, which still had its wooded background, descending almost to the shore, and its small colony of villas in leafy gardens. There, with her governess and friends, she enjoyed long walks, picnics on the shore and delightful rides through the cork and pine woods where the countryside was decked with roses and jasmine. The reverie ended, however, when her ailing father died, and she and her mother returned to America.

During the next twenty years she married, established herself as a novelist, and travelled frequently to England and continental Europe. In 1907, at the age of forty-five, she decided to spend her winters in Paris and acquired an apartment there. When the war broke out she was in England looking for a house to buy, but returned immediately to France because she wanted to help a country that had given her a great deal of support during the difficult years of her husband's mental breakdown. Throughout the war she worked tirelessly to help the orphans and refugees, for which she won the Legion d'Honneur. In 1919, when it was all over, she was feeling 'chilly and grown old', and went south for a four-month break to bask in the winter sunshine.

On one of the many picnics for which she became famous, she came across Ste Claire, a former convent within castle walls, perched high above the old town of Hyères. Here there were wonderful views across the plains to the Giens peninsula, and the Iles d'Or in the distance, which she described as 'floating on a silver sea'. Ste Claire became her Great Good Place, its twenty-eight terraces like stairways to Paradise. She called it her *cielo della quieta*, after Dante. Below it was La Solitude, the little house Robert Louis Stevenson had lived in, and Hyères, both much as he had described them, with fields of tuberoses and sheets of violets, all growing wild. Her lease was signed just before her sixtieth birthday, and she felt as if she was signing the parish register, 'being married to the right man at last'.

One of the first things she did was to bring the famous Monsieur Nabonnand, the 'roseriste' of Golfe Juan, to have a look. She recorded that he was 'in raptures about my series of terraces and the opportunity for growing camellias and gardenias besides all the roses that ever were'. She was longing for her niece, Beatrix Farrand, to come too. 'Oh what orgies we'll have on my twenty-eight terraces!' Less delirious was the reaction of the writer Carlo Placci, on taking in her labyrinthine terraces: 'But how very unsimple – how very, very unsimple!' This seemed to amuse her.

To Edith, overjoyed with the promise of things to come, those first blissful months spent planning and planting seemed like a long honeymoon. But it was not

A STATUESQUE EDITH WHARTON AT STE CLAIRE.

to last. A few days before she'd even moved in, just before Christmas, she wrote the first of many calamitous descriptions of severe gales and frost, her images crisp and salient. 'All gardens from Marseilles to Menton were wiped out. Black crapy rags angling woefully from denuded terraces . . . Even my splendid old caroube trees all frizzled and brown . . . I had a magnificent buddleya [sic] which covered one of my highest terrace walls and was just preparing to hang out its hundreds of yellow plumes – it is as bare as a ship's rigging in a gale! – and the only consolation people can find is that "it hasn't been known since 1870".' But on Christmas day she was still picking camellias and violets.

In 1921, she won the Pulitzer Prize for *The Age of Innocence* – it was the first time the prize had been awarded to a woman. The $1,000 prize came in handy, she said, to 'polish off the gardens at Ste Claire'; and when, eight years later, she was able to buy the property outright, she had earned the money to do it with what she called her 'littery works'.

Digging herself in at Hyères from November to May every year, she wrote, she 'received', she 'pottered' about in the garden; fussing and fretting over her earthbound charges and talking to them in 'nursery talk', as if they were children. Finally she had the long-awaited visit from, Beatrix, who had helped her lay out the gardens at The Mount, and who had designed the Princeton and Yale campuses and the Byzantine-inspired Dumbarton Oaks garden in Washington DC, which so impressed Stravinsky that he set it to music. Together they strolled around the terraces, and Edith asked Beatrix to fill in some 'gaps', sparking off much lively correspondence. After 'Trix' has sent her gladioli and irises from America, Edith reports: 'We are warming ourselves at the glow of your gladioli – a clos vougeot red, the velvetiest and richest I ever saw'. She shares an amusing description of a lily in a Dutch catalogue: '"When their bottoms are opened they become rosy." Well they may!' Another time, 'the oncocyclus iris family are not faring well: 'only one little wizened William survives and Frieda far from robust, and another onco iris which is likewise busily dying. I'm afraid I cannot induce him to remain with me.'

By 1928 she had bought the whole hill of straggling olives and aloes. These, with the grey rock, she used as backgrounds for her plantings, that were never allowed to dominate the natural beauty of the site. Along the drive a broad band of purple irises grew against the buttresses blue with kennedya. The hillside to the east of the house was planted with many fine specimens of shrubs, Judas trees and double crimson cherries. Her rock garden of sub-tropical plants, cacti and succulents was reputed to be even more complete than that of the Prince of Monaco! Her terraces all had themes – an orangery, a rose garden, a spring garden of cherries and daffodils, a tall pergola rising out of a bed of tulips and blue violas – and every nook and cranny filled with rare or native plants.

Her pride and joys in November were the two 'mandarins', the glorious 'daisy tree' (*Dahlia imperialis*), and montonoa. A 'perfect December in bloom' included violets, snapdragons, irises, marigolds, agatheus, biennial echiums, passiflora, camellias and mimosa. In 1928 she dismissed her gardener, Simon, for being dishonest and neglectful, and although the weather was fine it was because of him, she said, that she had no flowers that year. Replaced by Joseph, the brother-in-law

A VIEW THROUGH MARGUERITES, OSTEOSPERMUM AND LAVENDER OF THE OLD CHURCH THAT FORMED THE BOUNDARY OF HYERES IN WHARTON'S DAY.

of Charles de Noailles' butler, who had been to the Ecole de Versailles and was wonderful, the list resumes. By 1930, daturas and bougainvillaea had been added to the list. March brought wisteria, tulips, tree peonies, irises, Judas trees, choisya, early pale echiums, *Clematis armandii*, peaches and cherries in blossom, rose hedges. In April of 1933, *'Malus aldenhanii*, a sight for the Gods'.

Despite contributing advice to Mrs Philip Martineau's *Gardening in Sunny Lands*, the vicissitudes of the climate continued to defeat her. Sublime weather was served up on a 'golden salver', otherwise it was 'the Furies and their little arrangements'. In a letter to Bernard Berenson she commiserated with him over the loss of his cypress trees: 'It's no use being uplifting about it as people were with me over the caroubes,' she wrote grimly. 'The Furies know their job, and generally do it thoroughly.' All the minutiae of weather, from dramatic drops in temperature to droughts, were recorded. Every February was 'worst' than the last, and the next worse than the worst of the worst. She had a symbiotic relationship with it, as she did with anything that she cared about or that was suffering around her – she was devoted to her maids and dogs – and every loss was felt very deeply. In 1929, snowstorms and howling, blinding gales devastated her garden, virtually wiping it out. A physical *contrecoup* followed, with pneumonia and palpitations which lasted ten days. She was so dangerously ill, she nearly died. Can one love a garden so much, she asked, that 'my old fibres should have been so closely interwoven with all these roots and tendrils.'

ECHIUMS, SUCH AS THESE AT STE CLAIRE, ADORN MANY PROTECTED RIVIERA GARDENS IN SPRING.

She described herself as a 'rooted and possessive person', and was famous for her extraordinary energy; people 'bowed' before it. Many people found her intimidating, formal and stiff – as upright, as the French would say, 'as if she had swallowed an umbrella' – and she was famous for her 'iron mitt'. First impressions were inevitably unfavourable – even the Berensons, as Mary noted in her diary, at first 'clearly hating her', found her reserved and severe. If she didn't like you, it was said, she would freeze you out, but once you had gained her respect she was, by all accounts, a most generous and loyal friend. Lady Aberconway (Cristabel of Bodnant) said her curiosity about things and people surpassed even that of Virginia Woolf. 'She stimulated everyone, I want Edith as my friend.' A friend, Philomène, spoke of 'all the warmth beneath the snow'. She had a constant stream of visitors, and described her life as one of 'gardening, writing and receiving without pause'. Only the gardening and the writing were passions that never palled. When three bouts of flu left her as weak as a cat, on cotton wool legs, she was still rhapsodizing about the heavenly capricious spring weather, with the garden tuning up here and there like a symphony orchestra and suddenly bursting into a glorious *tutti*. Socializing tired her out, and eventually she was ordered to take it 'homeopathically'; whereupon she observed: 'Certainly it is a bore to have to take in sail, when one has had the freedom of the high seas for so many years.'

In April, her little Peke, Linky, died, leaving Edith devastated – 'face to face for the first time in my life,' she said, 'with real loneliness; my

THE TERRACE AT STE CLAIRE AS IT IS TODAY: MINUS THE PLANE TREES.

last link with all my dear past – what a train of ghosts will follow her little burial today.' A month later Edith's very old friend Lady Elcho died, and by August she had joined her. Johnnie Johnston came up from Menton for her funeral, Kenneth Clark was one of her pallbearers, and she was buried in Versailles. After her death, Robert Norton, who had been with her when she first discovered Ste Claire on one of their famous picnics, wrote of her gardens: 'What a great personality emerges from them all.'

THE TERRACE AT STE CLAIRE
AS IT WAS IN THE 1920S WHEN
EDITH WHARTON LIVED THERE
AND WROTE UNDER THE
PLANE TREES.

Parc St Bernard and Villa Noailles

CHARLES DE NOAILLES

When Charles de Noailles died at his home in Grasse at the age of ninety, he was still making plans for his *potager*. He had been gardening on the Riviera since 1924, almost but not quite as long as Norah Warre. Charles was to gardening on the Riviera in the twentieth century what Sir Thomas Hanbury, 'The Lord God of these parts', had been in the nineteenth. He devoted his life to beauty and originality, marrying his love of ideas with his love of plants. He had begun by planting unsuitable and brightly coloured bulbs under cork oaks in the *maquis* high up at Hyères, and ended up the master plantsman, his garden a distillation of all that he had absorbed in his long aesthetic life – what he liked, what suited, what wanted to grow. He brought both novelty and wisdom, and he thought of the garden in all its dimensions: the sound and smell of a garden as well as the look of it.

He also thought about people. For thirty years a door remained open for anyone caring to step in, an act of trust and generosity unheard of in a nation that jealously guards its privacy with high walls and double-locked gates. When his plumber got married, he told the young bride that she could help herself to whatever she liked in the garden to start her own. 'What do I say if someone sees me?' she asked. 'Just show them these,' he said – handing her his distinctive pair of silver secateurs.

Then there is the story of the children who stole his apples. The old head gardener, Pierre Cespuglio, who was nearly seventy, threatened to bring them up before the Vicomte but was never fast enough to catch them. One day he successfully scooped them up and, taking them by the scruff of the neck, brought them to the Vicomte. 'Oh, so you like my apples and pears?' he said. 'Well you can have as many as you want, only the next time, come and ask me for them.' He had that sense of curiosity which characterizes all great minds, travelling hundreds of kilometres out of his way to see a plant or flower he had never seen before. He was also a

VICOMTE CHARLES DE
NOAILLES UNDER THE JUDAS
TREE PERGOLA AT VILLA
NOAILLES IN GRASSE.

gardener with vision and faith: he planted with great joy plants and trees that he knew he would never see flower.

Charles de Noailles had the prestigious distinction of being elected one of the few non-English Vice Presidents of the Royal Horticultural Society – a rare distinction for people who aren't English – as well as President of the International Dendrological Society. To Pippa Irwin, who used to see him at Norah Warre's, he was quite simply 'the most elegant man I've ever met'.

The earliest recollection of Charles de Noailles's interest in gardening comes from an account of him in a book by Victor Hugo's grandson, who described him growing annuals in the trenches during the First World War. Soon after the war he married Marie Laure, the great-granddaughter of the Marquis de Sade and the daughter of Madame de Croisset, who gave Ferdinand Bac his first commission, re-designing her villa and gardens in Grasse in the Spanish style. Villa Noailles was a wedding present from her, while Parc St Bernard was a present from Charles's mother, the Princess de Poix, whom Edith Wharton has described as one of the 'two most radioactive women I know'. She looked after their garden in Fontainebleau, so, to all intents and purposes, the Parc was Charles's first real garden.

It did not get off to a promising start. Initially all the energy went into building this cubist Mallet-Steven house which everyone thought was marvellous except for Henri Perrot, the major-domo who christened it '*grand cabanan au bord de mer pour gens riches*' and complained that

LIKE AN ACTRESS IN A RENAISSANCE PLAY, THIS LADY IN STONE ADDRESSES A GENTLEMAN BUST IN A GARDEN ROOM CREATED AS AN EXERCISE IN SYMMETRY. RISING UP BEHIND IS A HUGE AESCULUS FLAVA.

VIEW OF THE OLD TOWN OF
HYERES FROM PARC ST
BERNARD DESIGNED AND
PLANTED BY PIERRE QUILLIER.
ON THE LEFT A LAVENDER
HYBRID, MONIQUE CUCHE,
GREY SANTOLINA AND WHITE
FLOWERING JUDAS TREES.

the rooms were too small, there were endless stairs and no lift; it was *crevant*. The house became and still is – along with Eileen Gray's house in Roquebrune – much talked about as people began to hear about the outside bedroom with the *lit suspendu* hung from the ceiling inside sliding glass doors, where Man Ray shot his *Les Mystères du Château Du Dé* financed by Charles, and Luis Bunuel's *L'Age d'Or*, for which Charles was threatened with excommunication and banned from the Jockey Club.

Originally built as a small villa, it attracted so much attention that all their friends kept inviting themselves along to stay, so they added more rooms and, being *très sportifs*, a swimming pool and a squash court – and showers. With their water supply already restricted, the garden took second place to the social demands of the house.

The most famous tiny garden on the coast, designed by Guevrekian, first appeared at the 1925 Decorative Arts Exposition in Paris, where it was seen by Charles and Marie Laure. Charles thinking of a triangular spot where it would fit nicely, ordered one. Ganay compared it to the prow of a boat, and it was planted with spiky agaves which associated well with the architectural starkness of the house. Charles now began buying up bits of terraces as they became available below the original ramparts of the property – nibbling land, as Henri Perrot describes it – and annexing them to the garden. The terraces had almond trees, olives and chick peas which had been there forever and grew by themselves with no help from any one.

Whereas Mrs Wharton employed a head gardener – Henri's brother-in-law, as it happens – here Charles was head gardener, and was sorely disappointed with his efforts. Longing to grow his temperate English favourites, he was stuck with a terrain that had no water, no earth; that was protected in winter, but in summer was a real oven – everything 'cooks and burns'. It was a *terre ingrat* – and here, according to his major-domo, *il s'est fait la main*.

He succeeded well with the Nabonnand rose General Schablikine, a hybrid of Mutabilis, which he said was good for any terrain, and the evergreen oaks he imported from Italy were 'the most happy plantings'. It seems he could only grow there the plants he didn't like much – the 'papery flowers', such as cistus and abutilons, or succulents, which he didn't much care for either. What he longed for was to be able to grow the plants he had seen growing in English gardens.

Finally, after the war, in 1947 he gave up. Leaving Marie Laure on the Hyères hilltop, he went to their house in Grasse to plant the most elegant magnolias, davidias, halesias, cornus, camellias and tree peonies. She remained the great patroness of the *avant-garde*. They spoke to each other every day on the phone, and when she died in 1970 he invited all her friends to come and take what they wanted from the house, and then sold it to the town of Hyères. It is now under the imaginative direction and care of the major-domo's grandson, Pierre Quillier who is making the most of the dry conditions by concentrating on acquiring interesting collections of Mediterranean plants.

THE WINTER AND SPRING FLOWERING BORDER AT PARC ST BERNARD. OLIVE TREES ARE UNDERPLANTED WITH A LONG BANK OF ASPERETUS WITH DIMORPHOTHECA, OSTEOSPERMUM, AND LANTANA SELLOWIANA.

After years of trying to get his desert at Hyères going, it must have been heaven for Charles to be in Grasse, where he had an abundant supply of water and could squeeze no more than six into his dining-room for lunch! He enjoyed showing people around, always taking the same route. He purposely made the paths very narrow, only fifty centi-metres across, so that one walks in single file, each person experiencing this garden of wonder and surprises alone.

A couple of years before he died he wrote a book with Roy Lancaster called *Mediterranean Gardens* which he was meant to expand on in a second volume into which he would put his thoughts and experiences of many years of gardening. That book was never written. He did, however, impart a great deal of his garden wisdom to Pierre Schneider, for an article in *Vogue*, wisdom that deserves a permanent place be-tween hard covers:

If you look at gardens created by Le Nôtre, the supreme authority on the French garden, you will see that what is on one side of an axis always balances what is on the other side, but that the two are never identical. It is the mediocre imitators who insist on rigid symmetry. I like patterns strongly stated by means of neatly kept low hedge borders: they constitute the architecture of the garden. But, within this formal framework, I like the plants and flowers to grow freely, as they please.

Statues are an excellent thing in the garden. They are half way be-tween man and matter, a perfect intermediary between nature and humanity. A true gardener is a sculptor as much as a painter. Any-way, the real painter, the real colourist is not he who relies on colours that are beautiful per se, but he who creates beautiful relations between colours that, in themselves, may be quite banal.

Nor should one be obsessed by one's eyes at the expense of one's other senses. Smell, for instance. It isn't as easy as it seems. The point of a scent is to be smelled. The trouble is that you cannot remain aware of it more than a few seconds. Hence the whole art consists in placing nice smelling plants at strategic points, where they take you by surprise. But if you pause and sit down, the effect wears off. With a little plan-ning, you can have three or four spots in your garden the year round where you suddenly exclaim, 'Heavens, what a nice smell!' But of course, the planning mustn't be noticeable.

Sound is by no means a negligible factor either. Much of the charm of fountains stems from the water's rustle. Trees, too, make different sounds. A friend of mine planted some aspens along the side of his house because they shiver audibly when no wind is blowing. People should always put a chatty tree in their garden.

A bad garden reflects its proprietor's wealth; a good one, his person-ality.

Having 'the green thumb', as the English say, may simply consist in sensing what plants desire. It is hard to explain, but I know that plants don't forgive you if you are not present when they are going through the labour of breaking into blossom. When I'm not in my garden at the time a plant I like is about to blossom, I feel very uneasy. I think I am being unfair to it.

Plants must be loved by their owners. For a man who has a very beautiful garden tended by ten gardeners, plants are things he sees in passing: they are not friends. But if a true gardener plants everything himself, there are some plants, certain trees, for instance, that he will never really see. Strange as it may seem, no gardener ever feels frus-trated by this. When I plant something ten inches tall, knowing it will eventually grow to be ten feet tall, I really see it in its full height. Besides, one does witness some growth. Then I tell myself: I have lost a few hairs, but it has gained a few branches. Considerable pleasures, these. And I assure you I am not in the least upset by the knowledge that my garden will really be seen in its full glory only by my great-grandchildren. In my garden at Grasse, I planted a Magnolia cam-bellii. I rejoice at the thought of it blossoming. To see it in flower, I calculated that I would have to live to be about a hundred and fifteen years old. Yet it is as if I did see it.

The garden has now passed into the hands of his grandson and name-sake, the young Charles de la Haye Jousselin, who is not only enjoying the magnolias but, inspired by the sober and delicate spirit of his grand-father, has paid homage to him by improving and reworking the Jardin à la Française. This was one of Charles's last projects before he died, in which he used balls of box to play games with perspective. Although the garden had been well looked after by the family in the decade fol-lowing Charles's death, the amount of construction higher up the hill dried up the water supply and plants were inevitably lost.

THE COLUMN IS A COPY OF ONE AT THE VILLA ALDOBRANDINI FRASCATI. THE UNDULATING HEDGE, INSPIRED BY HIDCOTE, SHELTERS THE COLLECTION OF TREE PEONIES. THE CYPRESS IS A SYMBOL OF GOOD LUCK.

Two years ago, Jane Harvey, a soft-spoken American, then studying garden design and restoration in England, met Charles's son-in-law, Bernard de la Haye Jousselin, who asked her to take charge of Villa Noailles when the family decided to restore and reopen the garden to the public. Living and working in the garden nearly every day, she finds it is a garden that takes you unawares, so well chosen are the plants for their colour, texture and fragrance; their berries and flowers. For her the garden is 'a very peaceful place. There is an air of calm and tranquillity in which one can feel the spirit of the person who created it.' Completely dedicated to the garden, she is helped by Bruno Goris. 'We go beyond what Charles de Noailles did, but not *outside* of what he would have done. Had he lived here all year round he would have planted for each season.' In fact, during the last three years of his life, Charles did spend the summers in Grasse and planted lagerstroemias and oleanders in a garden that before had been planted exclusively for winter and spring. Now they are very much aware that if the garden is to be open to the public, visitors will naturally want interesting plants to look at in summer as well. Judicious and sensitive planting for summer interest is being undertaken, in which the aim is to be faithful to the 'spirit' and character of the garden – by selecting plants 'le Vicomte' would have chosen himself. Bruno and Jane have picked up on his choice of *Salvia farinacea*, for example, and added other salvias that flower in summer. Gardens, after all, aren't like houses, that can be

A LARGE FIG TREE, STILL BARE IN EARLY SPRING, PERMITS A GLIMPSE OF THE WEEPING PRUNUS YEDOENSIS.

petrified and turned into museums, but places where life is continually evolving, often the passion of one person. Towards the end of his life Charles became quite handicapped and had ramps built everywhere, possibly because of his wheelchair. 'When you have a garden like this, you don't stay in bed just because you don't want to go out in a wheel-chair,' remarks Bruno. 'I too would go out – on all fours if necessary.'

Charles de la Haye Jousselin, Jane Harvey and Bruno Goris are all deploying their special talents to maintain and develop the classic beauty, fine plantsmanship and generosity of spirit that characterized the garden of the Vicomte de Noailles.

IN A DESIGN TYPICAL OF THE 1940S, THIS CORNER IS DIVIDED INTO COMPARTMENTS EACH THICKLY PLANTED WITH A DIFFERENT VARIETY SUCH AS CHEIRANTHUS, NERINES, AMARYLLIS BELLADONNA AND THE PURPLE-LEAVED BERGENIA. THE ALLIUMS SEEDED THEMSELVES, AND SEEN HERE IS CONVOLVULUS CNEORUM. OVERHANGING THE SCENE IS AN ARBUTUS UNEDO GRAFTED ONTO AN ARBUTUS ANDRACHNOIDES WHICH TOLERATES ACID SOIL BETTER.

Chapter Four
CONTEMPORARY GARDENS

———— • ————

T HE IDEA PUT FORWARD BY THE LANDSCAPE ARCHITECTS earlier this century, that a garden should blend in with views of the mountains and sea, and merge with natural vegetation, is a thing of the past. The modern gardener on the Riviera is faced with an almost unrecognizable landscape, with buildings and congested roads intruding on once idyllic coastal views. In the *arrière-pays* and Provence the lines of pylons run like giant scars across land and landscape – to say nothing of the advancing armies of Leyland cypress. The old gardens are disappearing under concrete, rare and special plants with them. Many of the surviving gardens have been truncated; their budgets even more so. Nevertheless these challenges and the immense variety of plants available makes it a very exciting time to be gardening. Water has always been crucial. The first question is always '*L'eau, il y en a?*' – and when water has been found, they say it takes three generations to master the art of applying it. The use of colour is also much discussed; it is an area in which people are still unsure of themselves, and nervous of the slightest deviation from traditional rules.

Long gone are the days when Consuelo Balsan would advance across her terraces scattering bulbs, a team of gardeners following behind all on their knees with trowels, to plant them where they fell – for the sake of a natural effect. Sociological and economic changes have meant that gardens have to be managed practically and economically; glorious La Garoupe, for example, is maintained by two gardeners, where once there were twenty-five. The cost of living is so high now no one can afford to cosset temperamental plants that don't perform, except for real plantsmen like William Waterfield, who devotes most of his time to his rare collections. Bruno Goris will try three or four times with a plant before giving up – if it doesn't grow there are plenty of others that will. What puzzles Bruno is the way that people who live in the north want to grow plants that only grow in the south, and vice versa; the Parisians want to grow Mediterranean plants, the Mediterraneans want exotics, and on the Equator gardeners hanker after violets and daisies. However, people are finding that the indigenous or acclimatized 'natives' will thrive, and withstand frosts and droughts, and a repertoire of such plants is finding its way into more and more gardens.

GARDENS ARE NOW CREEPING TOWARDS THE BASE OF THE LIMESTONE RANGE KNOWN AS THE PENITENTS. EVEN HERE, THE PURITY OF THE LANDSCAPE IS THREATENED.

Gardening, like painting or writing, is a lifelong business; a continual honing and perfecting of one's art. As the French garden writer Giles Clement said, 'If someone thinks his garden is finished, it means it's dead.' The cosmopolitan nature of the Riviera is exemplified by the next four gardens, all made within the last fifteen years by people who positively *revel* in their gardens. Bruno Goris is Belgian; Cécile Chancel is French, but lives in England; Claus Scheinert is German; while Lulu de Waldner, with one parent Scottish and the other French, considers herself English! Each of the gardens is landscaped on terraces made unique by an inspired blend of pragmatism, passion and personality.

THE NABONNAND ROSE PAPA GAUTIER GROWS IN THE FOREGROUND, AND CHARD FROM THE POTAGER LIES ON THE TABLE. THE RARE ABUTILON MORANDIA OVERHANGS THE STONE BASIN BY THE WINDOW.

L'Oustaou dei Bailea

BRUNO GORIS

The aptly named Chemin du Paradis, a narrow path that would test the agility of an alpine goat, leads to an extraordinary gem of a garden hugging the mountainside in the clouds above Grasse. Here, in a little house built originally for the use of shepherds during the summer trans-

humance of sheep from the scorched pastures of the plains to higher, cooler meadows, lives Bruno Goris.

The place was discovered after the war by Bruno's grandfather. Exhausted by his efforts in North Africa and his time in the concentration camps, he took early retirement from the Belgian army and came to Grasse to convalesce. While taking a constitutional *promenade* on the hills, he came upon a terraced grove of three hundred orange trees and forty-five olives, and was so seduced by the view that he promptly bought the land.

He lost all but one of his orange trees in the catastrophic winter of 1956, but lived there all year round from 1957 onwards, cultivating his remaining olives. Bruno and his two brothers came for holidays, somewhat reluctantly, as the grandfather was difficult and authoritarian. 'I am told,' Bruno grins, 'that we resemble each other more and more.' Towards the end of his life, when he could no longer manage the stairway to 'paradise', he moved to the village, and gave Bruno his gardening tools. On his death, the house stayed empty for several years.

Although Bruno had always wanted to be a gardener, he was pushed into teaching by his parents. They thought him rather lazy, failing to realize that he was one of those children who exist in a vegetative state until they discover something which interests them. They imagined he thought that desultorily dead-heading roses was all there was to gardening. So he taught in a Belgian primary school, where he found

CAMPANULA LATIFOLIA AND THE ROSE CECILE BRUNNER GROW AT AN ALTITUDE OF 250 METRES WITH THE MANY-HUED MOUNTAIN IN THE BACKGROUND.

himself challenged by the children to engage their interest and stimulate their imaginations, and thus gained experience that would come in useful with his more conservative gardening clientele. He was still living at home, nursing his mother through a long and difficult illness, but whenever he could he escaped to this little house on the hill. It became his haven. When Bruno's parents both died within two years of each other, and he realized he could not afford to maintain homes in two countries, he cut his ties with Belgium and moved south. He arrived with his sofa, weighing one hundred kilos, and it took four men to carry it to the house, which he says was a memorable sight – like an 'enormous snail with eight legs'. In the beginning he did odd jobs on the Côte d'Azur then, being an excellent cook, he worked in a restaurant, and there met Norah Warre's great friend Pippa Irwin. She was a regular customer, and they would talk about plants until late in the evening. Bruno absorbed much gardening knowledge from their talks, and he now looks after the gardens at Villa Roquebrune, Norah Warre's former home.

Bruno's garden has achieved so many dimensions that it is easy to forget that the infrastructure supporting this luxuriant jungle is only a terraced hilly terrain, like all the others. The garden began not as a passion but as a garden '*pour mes besoins*', which meant a *potager* and fruit trees. The first thing he did, however, was replace the lime tree traditionally planted in front of old houses, which his grandfather, believing it attracted mosquitoes, had felled.

After the lime, he planted fruit trees: cherries, apricots and plums, positioned for easy pollination. The garden is almost ideally situated, facing south-east, protected from the mistral, and well watered by the proximity of the one thousand four hundred metre high mountain across the valley, which traps the clouds, producing rain and *petits vents coulis*. However, nothing is ever perfect, and chilly gales rush down the mountain gorges several times a year, cutting down the taller, more fragile plants.

BELOW: PRUNUS AVIUM, KNOWN AS THE ENGLISH CHERRY, GROWS IN THE UPPER REACHES OF THE GARDEN AMONG HAREBELLS BROUGHT BY BRUNO. GOLDEN HENGE BEGINS WITH HYPERICUM HIDCOTE.

RIGHT: ANOTHER CHERRY TREE HANGS ACROSS THE OSTRYA HEDGE IN THE POTAGER. A BORDER OF GREY SANTOLINA NEAPOLITANUM WAS PLANTED BECAUSE IT SHINES IN THE DARK SO BRUNO CAN FIND HIS CHARD!

Bruno had not left the fertile plains of Flanders to live on a scrubby hillside entirely devoid of green grass, and so he made himself a lawn in front of the house. Otherwise, there was no plan. 'I've noticed that everyone who starts off doing a plan always ends up changing it. Something always goes wrong – the colour, the height, nothing works out as expected.' So he started bit by bit, filling the front terrace closest to the house with plants he found growing wild, like cistuses, or others received as gifts.

He had read in an old book that *Ostrya carpinifolia* is better suited to the Mediterranean than hornbeam, so up went the ostrya hedges in the *potager*. It was divided into four compartments, according to traditional rotation methods, and protected from a whistling east wind by a hedge of rosemary. The demands of the household kitchen soon exceeded the capacity of the first terrace alone, so this was turned into an area for fast cropping salads and tomatoes, while the terrace below was devoted to the slower crops – potatoes, onions,

PLANTED ON AN OLD
REPOSITORY OF STONES ARE
PURPLE-LEAVED SAGE AND
YELLOW PHLOMIS, WHICH
DON'T NEED MUCH SOIL OR
WATER. A TELEPHONE LINE
RUNS ACROSS THE GARDEN IN
THE ECCENTRIC FRENCH
STYLE.

strawberries, peas and beans. He is presently on his third *potager* terrace, planted with artichokes, gooseberries, dahlias and cut flowers for
the house. There is still room for another six terraces should he need
them – which he surely will!

Above the *potager*, yet another six terraces rise up the hill. 'There was
nothing but olive trees and grass initially, and I found I couldn't mow
neatly along the wall, so I began by dividing a large clump of stachys a
client had discarded and planted bits of it all along the wall so as not to
damage the mower. Then I put in an abutilon and other bits and pieces
to aerate the base of the olives, which otherwise would have choked on
grass. The borders are so wide now that the path is barely penetrable.
On the top terrace I kept a large patch of grass as a counterpoint to all
this *fouilli*.'

As a plantsman and a colourist, Bruno is both sensitive and sensible
about colours. Like all creative artists, however, he is always evolving
and widening the rather narrow confines of 'good taste', which has
static, if not diminishing, returns. He arrived from Belgium brain-
washed by the pronouncements of the magazine *Ma Maison, Mon
Jardin*, but as he began to know the plants, his view broadened. The
'taste war' is most often fought over the use of colour in a garden.
People who are happy to paint their dining-rooms bright yellow or dec-
orate their homes with reds or oranges will banish them from the
garden. 'I was afraid to use colour in the beginning. I'd always loved
colour, but thought it was too violent. First came the yellow abutilon, a

plant I like very much, and little by little I began to weave in plants like phlomis and hemerocallis. There were plants that I found, was given or looked for to complete the gamut, and I began to weave them in, adding others to complete the range.'

Bruno's great passion is old-fashioned roses. 'I would start with a rose and associate three plants around it to lighten or complement it. There was one area that was supposed to be pink and white, but other things crept in among them. Red got in there with the *Rosa chinensis sanguinea* and *Gruss au Duplitz*, which I love very much, so a range of reds came into it.' Interspersed everywhere are the silvers and the violaceous colours – purplish blues which, together with the silver foliage, make the transitions. Bruno created his garden by trying out plants that he liked, adopting an impressionistic or pointillistic approach to accommodate the ranges of colour. The further you get from the house, the more striking and original are the colour combinations – not the least of which is 'Rose Henge'. Still at the preparatory stage, it is a homage to the sun in orange and yellow, dedicated to Aquarius (his birth sign), who pours water from the fountain of knowledge.

The spiky plants – the agaves, aloes, palms and cacti – have no place here, but he grows many 'exotics', notably the Holboellia which everyone expected to fail but which even survived the frosts of 1985.

He uses very little fertilizer on his plants, so they can take a few years to establish, and the humus problem is eased by letting the leaves drop

ROSA LA SEVILLIANA AND A CURLED UP CAT IN ONE OF MANY HIDDEN CORNERS OF BRUNO'S GARDEN.

off – except, of course, those with black spot or mildew. Bruno used to make his own compost, but because of thieves and gun-happy hunters the poultry have to be locked in when he is out, so now the kitchen waste goes directly to the poultry enclosures and is recycled through them.

Already something of a *folklorique* figure, inseparable from either his straw hat or his dog Cléome, Bruno can be found every year at the Foire des Plantes in Nice. There he displays, among other roses, his collection of locally bred Nabonnand roses which are his special interest. His love and knowledge of all plants, his capacity for listening to his clients while broadening their perspectives, and treating each garden on its own merits, have made Bruno Goris the most sought-after gardener on the Riviera. The highest compliment he can pay to a garden, whatever its style or colour, is that it has a soul. It's an elusive thing to define, but easy to recognize, and those who make the trek up to this eagle's nest will find, not only a garden with soul, but also a man poised to take over the reins of Charles de Noailles.

La Casella

CLAUS SCHEINERT AND TOM PARR

OLIVE TREES ARE UNDERPLANTED WITH A SEA OF AGAPANTHUS IN A STUDY OF BLUE AND SILVER.

Tom Parr and Claus Scheinert bought La Casella in 1983, an enclave of various cottages and a substantial villa on two and a half acres of land previously cultivated for jasmine. The house had been built in the 1960s by the architect Robert Streitz – a disciple of the Italian Emilio Terry – as a neoclassical replica of the Pavillon de Pompadour designed by Gabriel in Fontainebleau. It was obvious from the start that Claus wasn't going to be masterminding the decoration of the interior, as Tom Parr is the chairman of the prestigious design company Colefax and Fowler. Having given up his career as a Munich businessman, Claus found himself 'living on the Riviera with nothing to do'. Meanwhile, the garden lay there abandoned, but Claus didn't think of tackling it himself. He had no intention of doing it, nor did he think himself capable of the job, and so Russell Page was drafted in to help. Without actually seeing the garden, Page suggested something rather nice but impractical, and then died.

Enlisting the help of their friend Rory Cameron, a border at the front of the villa was filled with typically English perennials. By the end of May, however, all the flowers were finished for the year. In search of inspiration and knowledge they went to see the great Riviera gardens, including Chèvre d'Or, Villa Noailles and La Garoupe. Gradually Claus became more interested. Meanwhile, Tom and their many houseguests continued bringing plants from England, and Claus watched how they were planted. One day, he rather tentatively bought his first convolvulus and planted it next to their imports. The convolvulus died – whereas the English plants needed a lot of watering, the convolvulus didn't. Enough was enough. In his pragmatic way, Claus said to him-

self: 'Too many cooks. No more English. I do it myself' – after all, his father had been awarded a doctorate in agriculture.

For the better part of the next six years Claus did nothing else but garden. He read all the books and went to see all the gardens. When he had seen enough to know what he wanted, the local nurseries were plundered. Because he had never gardened before, there were no pre-conceptions, no preferences, no prejudices. He wanted neither an English garden, a German garden nor a French garden. He didn't want lots of different plants, just plants that would perform – an exterior to match Tom's interior. Slowly a frame of Jamesian 'verdant verdurous-ness' began to form around the ochre villa.

Most Riviera gardens were designed and planted for spring and autumn, but they had decided to live there all year round, so the challenge that presented itself was how to make the garden look alive and interesting throughout the year: what Edith Wharton had called 'a charm independent of the seasons, a thing of beauty all the year round'.

With no overall plan in mind, Claus had 'started on the terraces, one after the other. I looked around the gardens here to see what they had, and I planted that, because I knew it would do well.' At Villa Noailles, in Grasse, he particularly admired the formality of the winter garden combined with the informality of a summer planting. He also found much inspiration at the Chèvre d'Or. The Champins were as generous with their plants as with their advice, and jokingly referred to the

THE DECORATIVE SPOTS-IN-POTS TECHNIQUE ON THE TOP TERRACE WAS INSPIRED BY THE VILLA MARLIA IN ITALY, WHERE PLUMBAGO IS GROWN IN CONTAINERS. IT EFFECTIVELY COUNTERPOINTS THE TIGHTLY CLIPPED LAVENDER, BOX AND SANTOLINA.

Chèvre d'Or as 'the supermarket for the Claus Scheinert garden'. After two years' hard labour on his 'oeuvre', Nicole Champin sent the Association des Parcs Botaniques to La Casella. This group had been endlessly visiting the same five gardens for a number of years and wanted to see something new. Claus felt most honoured. 'Tom helped me with the colours, all pastels and no reds, oranges or yellows. You can quarrel about *rouge* in the heat – anyway, taste and colour I got from Tom, but the planting, I did.'

The main bones of the garden are evergreen: lawns, cypress hedges and olive trees providing a gamut of greens. Lesser bones are santolina, rosemary, lavender and acanthus, box and jasmine. Against this immutable background of green and silver, turns the palette of flowers: plumbago, roses like Schablikine and 'Lady Waterlow', echiums and romneyas, agapanthus and agrumes. Only the fruit trees, the oranges, lemons and cherries, present bold colour. Every once in a while the greenkeeper of the Opio golf course trims the lawns and paths to putting green perfection.

In winter the garden remains formal and neatly clipped; in summer it is a fresh green, with extra colour provided by a spots-in-pots technique. All year round there are spots of seasonal frivolity: pansies in winter, white tulips in March, followed by lilies – all dotted around in pots.

The 'rather nice' Russell Page suggestion had been to erect a pergola which would run the length of the Myrtle Walk, covered in plumbago

THE ULTIMATE IN JAZZY, POLISHED RIVIERA STYLE: WHITE ICEBERG ROSES, AGAPANTHUS IN POTS, LAVENDER, BOX, ORANGE TREES AND STONES. IT'S A COMBINATION OF STRONG GARDEN BONES WITH SUBDUED COLOURS.

and interspersed with lemon trees. Plumbagos and lemons, thought Claus, were a marvellous idea if one lived in the tropics, where plumbagos are evergreen, but in a Riviera winter 'you'd have the lemons, but it would basically look dead'. Also, the pergola would have cut the view from the salon along the main axis of the garden. 'I had to work very hard to dissuade Tom, because the tunnel was ordered and the plumbagos had already arrived.' Claus, recalling the Villa Marlia in Tuscany, planted them in pots instead.

Tom, meanwhile, having borne with fortitude the gradual, diplomatic, but nevertheless steady disappearance of the contents of his English border, was for the most part quite content to let Claus rush round doing the planting while he designed the stunning pebbled courtyard area.

This is a garden made by a man who, ten years ago, did not know 'the difference between a pansy and a tulip' – and didn't particularly want to know. Gradually, however, the garden crept into his life and, for many years, stole it. Its success is based on a few simple but essential principles and priorities. 'What I appreciate are local plants, in silvers, blues, whites and greens, which look good all year round. I stick to what I have and keep it healthy. If you extend too much, the gardeners have trouble keeping it up.' He has now been asked by several friends to help with what is termed '*le style* Claus Scheinert', which he defines as convenience and suitability.

AURUM LILIES AND FLAG IRISES IN THE SPRING GARDEN COMPLEMENT THE GOLDEN STONE OF AN OLD WELL DUG ABOUT A HUNDRED AND FIFTY YEARS AGO WHEN THE LAND WAS A JASMINE FARM.

Jas Crema
LULU DE WALDNER

Standing unperturbed in the middle of a Vaucluse garden facing Mont Ventoux is a life-size elephant, whose wrought-iron skeleton is clad in white *Clematis balearica* to make him beautiful in January, and yellow *Rosa banksiae* to do the same in May. For the rest of the year he remains a handsome, dependable green. Elsewhere in the garden stand several horses' heads, like chessboard knights, their bases covered in winter-flowering *Jasminum nudiflorum*, their heads awash with yellow *banksiae* in spring. Stones surround some of the trees, encircling carpets of flowers, and in the garden proper are two square beds containing nothing but strawberries. All this bears the unmistakable stamp of Lulu de Waldner, a woman of great originality and verve, whose forthright manner and quirky imagination have made her a legend in gardening circles for every garden she has made, she has made unique.

Lulu was born of an *entente cordiale* between a British father, Edward Esmond Valentine, and a French mother. Two sisters preceded her into this world, and she therefore had to hold her own. Also, drummed into her by her parents, was the dictum that one did things well or not at all.

Horses, dogs and family apart, flowers have been the great love of her life, and she has gathered them from the time she was small, in the gardens she knew in a childhood divided between Scotland and France.

PITTOSPORUM TOBIRA GIVES
THE GARDEN STRENGTH AND
THE BIG PLANE TREE LENDS IT
SHADE. AGAPANTHUS, SWEET
ALYSSUM AND THE
CENTREPIECE 'VASE' IN BOX
ARE TYPICAL OF LULU DE
WALDNER'S STYLE.

Her grandfather owned a château outside Paris, with a garden in which
each grandchild had a private patch; Lulu's was round. She began by
planting violets round the edge and, inside, bits and pieces of both
flowers and vegetables mixed together. 'I was always very fussy about
my garden; first I had scissors and then secateurs. In Scotland, my
mother cut the sweet peas and my father cut the roses – we called them
"snubblos", and I had them by my bed in vases as tiny as thimbles.'
Taught by governesses in Scotland until the age of ten, Lulu then went
to school in Paris. 'I was *Louisa l'Anglaise*; I had a blue coat, they had
grey coats; I had a ham sandwich, they had a *pain au chocolat*; and the
teacher used to say, in the arched, sonorous tones of *la vieille France*:
"*Les Anglais, avec leurs égoïsme insulaire, nous prirent le Canada et l'Inde.*" I
was laughed at and pointed at. But I didn't care, it didn't worry me.'

She married Baron Geoffroy de Waldner, and they lived with their
four babies in the Bois de Boulogne, separated only by a hedge of
yellow pyracantha from their neighbour – of all people, the writer Marcel Pagnol. Lulu's house was rather English, with three steps up to the
front door dominated by an enormous chestnut tree and a terrace of
crazy paving. In the cracks between the stones she planted tulips, then
surrounded the whole thing with curly kale – the ornamental cabbage
which is fashionable today, but was then quite original. The terrace
above was gay with geraniums, and behind it was a 'funny little
Wagnerian hill with rocks', packed with plants collected in the woods,
and others brought back from Chelsea, the Royal Horticultural Society

shows, and the trips she made with her husband to the Far East and India. She enjoyed collecting cuttings in Africa – until they were attacked by tribesmen. On being halted at French customs, laden with plants, her clothes in ruins, she would deflect the officer's enquiries with a resounding '*C'est bon pour la France*', and sweep past them.

Her husband Geoffroy owned race-horses at Chantilly, and to be closer to the stud farm they leased La Grange, a house in the country outside Mortefontaine which had once belonged to Napoleon's favourite sister, Pauline Borghese: it would be Lulu's home for thirty years. In the garden, lyrically designed and romantically planted, she created a very wide border of old roses and Victorian flowers, strictly in pinks, blues and whites, sloping down to a small lake on whose shores stood topiary swans in yew and topiary teddy bears in box. Later, she added something else entirely original, a 'chessboard garden' – twelve alternating flower and vegetable squares, each square surrounded by lavender. In spring, for example, green and white viridiflora tulips rose up from a floating bed of pink myositis, while the adjacent square would be planted with carrots or leeks, and so on. Her arrangements of roses and celery in a vase, among other domestic idiosyncrasies, were often recorded in *Vogue* magazine.

An old friend, Charles de Noailles, introduced her to the French Horticultural Society. A 'mania' for mixing things, often things just found in the woods, landed her the job of organizing the flower arrang-

A VENERABLE FIG TREE AFTER
A SPRING DOWNPOUR.

ing exhibits for the 1959 Paris Floralies, which was hailed as the 'Flower Show of the Century' – an episode she now regards as 'much too funny'. The flower arranging English arrived by boat, dripping with velvet and armed with ornaments and statues, which the French thought very ugly. The event attracted thousands of people, and the British Ambassador's wife, Lady Jebb, had her vase stolen – by whom, nobody will ever know. Every morning at seven Lulu would arrive with her old butler to sweep and tidy up. Lady Diana Cooper and Lady Duff came, Lady Eden and Lady Anne Tree were among the judges, and Russell Page designed the set piece for Vilmorin, the contemporary French equivalent of Hilliers.

Two years later, Lulu organized a flower arranging competition in every shop window of the fashionable Avenue Victor Hugo. It stretched for one thousand five hundred metres, all the way up to the Etoile. A princess, a dowager duchess and a marquise were reported in the *Figaro* to be standing in their stockinged feet, one countess *'toute de rose vêtue'*. Outside, the chauffeurs, local residents and passers-by crowded each shop window, all opinions and advice. 'La Baronne G. de Waldner,' wrote the reporter, *'très calme, arrangeait ses vases, tout en faisant face à une offensive telephonique ininterrompue.'* Madame André de Vilmorin walked away with first prize – a gold powder box. On the committee of the French Horticultural Society, Lulu tried unsuccessfully to organize something similar to the RHS Vincent Square shows, and the members would sit spellbound, listening to her reading, by the light of a little lamp, a lecture she had laboriously written out in longhand. *'Mesdames et Messieurs,'* she would begin, *'J'ai le grand honneur de vous parler aujourd'hui d'un sujet Passionnant . . . votre jardin d'été . . . .'*

In memory of her husband who died in 1970, Lulu planted several enormous topiary horses' heads at the entrance to the Evry racecourse, now so tall that a ladder is required to clip them. Soon afterwards the lease on La Grange ran out for good. Marcel Pagnol, still living on the other side of the yellow pyracantha in the Bois, had always said to her, 'You're quite mad to go to England and Scotland all the time. You were meant to live in Provence.' Lulu's friends and family, knowing it was inconceivable that she could live happily in the north of France without her horses, also suggested the sun.

She went south in search of a house, staying with Rory Cameron in Menerbes, but found nothing suitable and became fed up with looking. On the eve of her departure, a friend mentioned an agricultural property whose owners wanted a valuation, and that it might be, but probably wasn't, for sale. She asked to see it. What she saw was a three-hundred-year-old crumbling *bastide*, exposed to the elements, set in a rocky landscape, among rows of rolling vines and directly opposite a thirteenth-century castle crowning the hill-top village of Le Barroux. The vines came practically to the doorstep, and there was no garden at all. 'I'd keep it, if I were you,' Lulu remarked to the proprietor, 'but if you ever want to sell it, just remember that for me it is Paradise.' By 1979, Jas Crema was hers. Some time after the sale, Lulu bumped into the former proprietor. 'I never asked you about the water or the roof,' she said, and the proprietor replied, 'If you had, I never would have sold the house!' The roof had been rotten, and the wells dry. Several diviners were brought in, and one eventually succeeded in finding a

A COMPOSITION OF LINES: PATHS HEDGED WITH ROSEMARIES, AND ROWS OF OLIVES AND LAVENDER ZIG-ZAG ACROSS THE BOTTOM OF THE GARDEN.

supply of rather poor quality water – a hundred and thirty-four metres down. Lulu rerouted the avenue leading to the house, and in its place she made her garden, consisting broadly of three wide terraces proportionate to the size and shape of the *bastide*. The poor soil was vastly enriched with loam brought from a nearby farm which had recently been sold.

She was helped, she says, by her dear friend, the botanist Hiram Winterbottom, who advised her to plant China roses only; advice which stood her in good stead. But she laments the years she wasted – the 'nobody told me' years, three of which were spent busily looking for the wonderful white lagerstroemias seen growing 'shamelessly' round Biarritz, only to discover that they required an acid soil. The wrought-iron skeleton of the elephant was erected on the appointed spot, dressed with great enthusiasm in wild box, but 'passed out' two weeks later. The wild box was replaced with a cultivated variety, but this one grew too slowly. Lulu then had the idea of clothing it in *banksiae*, which she discovered could be pulled about and clipped just like box. It was an outstanding success, so she used it on her horses' heads as well.

During a dendrologist's tour of Ireland she fell in love with the startling *Passiflora quadrangularis*. One greenhouse alone houses an enormous collection of this species, growing ever larger with each yearly review of her specialist's list. Scented pelargoniums, many varieties of jasmine, and citrus in pots are sheltered in winter in the second greenhouse, alongside temperamental tropical plants brought back from her travels. Ladybird cushions, socks and brooches are everywhere, and another well-known idiosyncrasy is long rows of old-fashioned roses from her garden lined up in small vases underneath matching Fantin Latour-like paintings of them. 'A garden,' she says, 'is like the inside of a room – but outside and furnished.'

After many years, her taste in colours remains the same. 'I don't think you change very much. I don't do anything lavish any more, I have to do things that are practical now.' The stalwarts hold the garden together whatever the weather. Seasonal glories come and go – the irises, the agapanthus, all the best roses suffused throughout the garden – shown off but always framed by solid plant bones – the rosemary, pittosporum, box and oleanders – which for years have met the challenge posed by the baking sun and a drying, piercing mistral.

Where once was a sea of lavender, now run decorative ripples, integrated with a newly planted 'ancient' olive grove. This was something Lulu had always wanted, but which had been prohibitively expensive. Then one day, she had a windfall. A local grower took a fancy to apricots and sold all his olive trees to Lulu. Even the most ancient trees are quite easily moved and practically indestructible. The grove now looks as if it had been there for ever. After the olive harvest the fruit is pressed at the local mill, and the oil is much appreciated by family and friends.

Lulu says that as you get older, you simplify your life. Her constant companion now is Ben, the Dandie Dinmont terrier, affectionately known by all as 'Mummy's Ben'.

BELOW: MUMMY WITH HER BEN.

A GLIMPSE THROUGH THE
ENTRANCE GATES OF THE
POTAGER REVEALS LAVENDER,
SALVIA FARINACEA, SIMPLE
RED DAHLIAS, COURGETTES,
POTATOES AND BEANS. THE
HOLLYHOCKS IN THE
BACKGROUND ARE GROWN
FROM SEEDS BROUGHT FROM
ENGLAND.

VAL JOANIS

CECILE CHANCEL

Fifteen years ago, Val Joanis was an abandoned sixteenth-century *bas-tide* surrounded by three hundred and twenty hectares of fields and woods. Now it produces one million two hundred thousand bottles of wine annually from a hundred and ninety-two acres of vineyards, and its *potager à l'ancienne* is one of the best in France. Given to Seigneur de Joanis by the French king François the First in recognition of his stand against the Protestants, this garden flouts the popular opinion that flowers are impossible to grow in the capricious Provençal climate.

While living in the middle of Paris with a small garden, the Chancels bought Val Joanis in order to be able to accommodate all seven of their children under one roof. It had taken them five years to find a property which had both house and land; usually it was one without the other, but owning a vineyard was something businessman Jean Chancel had done before, and now wanted to do again. His wife, Cécile, had had a couple of demanding gardens and knew what she wanted to do. Born and brought up in a large townhouse in Aix-en-Provence, she also knew the climate well, and is as impervious to the sun as a native lizard. Decked out in a large hat, she will garden as comfortably under the scorching sun as an Englishman under an umbrella.

Cécile's first garden was by the sea, in Marseilles, and included the Mediterranean plants she couldn't grow in her father's garden in the colder Aix. Instead, she had salt and wind from the sea, and on days when the mistral blew, the garden was showered with oily seawater from the nearby refineries and looked *cuit comme une vieille salade*. She surrounded the garden in grey Atriflex, as a screen against the wind and pollution, trained figs palisaded against it, and filled the garden in with vines, laurels, arbutus, palms, phormiums and ivies.

On moving to Paris, her next garden was the exact opposite, entirely in the shade, and by demolishing workshops and two small buildings she recreated a medieval garden with ivies and other foliage plants. Val Joanis would be different again, but this time, rather than adapting, she had a plan. The first step was to try to imagine how a person living there in the seventeenth or eighteenth century would have gone about creating a *potager à l'ancienne*.

Starting from scratch, they chose a south-facing site, sheltered from the mistral, carved three terraces out of the hill and built the walls, using stone salvaged from a Roman ruin on the estate. While her husband was busy getting his vineyard established, she worked with the stonemason. When it was finished, and much admired, she showed it to an architect friend who thought it very fine – but wasn't there something missing? Nothing came to mind. Where were the stairs?

All the conditions which earn Provence its reputation as difficult and restrictive gardening country – bitter cold in winter, blazing heat in summer – prevailed here, except for the mistral, and it also had an

LAVENDER IN ALL ITS PROVENCE GLORY, BORDERED BY WHITE COSMOS ON THE RIGHT AND MALVA, DOUBLE FRENCH HOLLYHOCKS AND NICOTIANA SYLVESTRIS LIME GREEN ON THE LEFT.

unhelpfully high alkaline soil with a pH of 8.5. Experienced only in coastal and shade-loving patches, she brought in Tobbie Loup de Viane to help and advise on creating a *potager*, which at the time was the most unfashionable kind of garden in France; nobody was writing about them, and in the end she had to work it all out for herself with Tobbie's help, by trial and error. Logically, it seemed that cut flowers and vegetables should be on the first terrace, closest to the house, followed by flowers and roses on the second, and ornamental and fruit trees on the bottom one, to round it off. Whenever common sense and reason prevailed over fantasy, she and de Viane chose local plants, and for these she went to the best nursery on the Côte – Chez les Soeurs Schneider in Cannes, whose soil was the same as hers. She ordered practically everything from there. Mlle Paulette, one of the Schneider sisters, came to Val Joanis every spring and autumn for five consecutive years, and together they filled the garden with hundreds of plants.

Cécile brought her three terraces together by means of a seventy-metre long pergola bought from an old château in the next village. This had originally been built by the proprietor as a race-track for his ostriches – part of a large menagerie he had collected in Africa during the 1850s. It had been erected against a wall, so in order to complete the arch, the frame had to be extended by the local blacksmith. Cécile planted fragrant climbers such as honeysuckles, jasmines and English roses along the whole length of it. She also bought a *cage à loup* from this château for the dogs, but the extraordinary Japanese gazebo which remains her heart's desire, shaped like a Chinese hat with three small bells on the roof, still eludes her. Just as the owner was about to sell, he changed his mind. She goes twice a year for tea, and to court him; '*Cher monsieur,*' she begins, 'about this gazebo . . . ', but each time he says no. Everything has long been in place for its arrival, the circle marked out, the surrounding border already planned with *Rhamnus alaternus*, Italian buckthorn. Ten years she's been waiting, and it may be another ten, but in the end, says Cécile, '*Je l'aurais.*'

Old established gardens are invaluable sources of ideas and plants; a glimpse over an old wall, or through a rusty gate, will often reveal something she likes – in which case she stops and asks. In this way she discovered the rarely seen but very beautiful *Clerodendron trichotomum*. She ordered yellow, but an orange one arrived, and as she dislikes orange, she cut all its flowers off for the first year. Then, when she noticed that everything else flowering in early September was in very pale colours and that this orange clerodendron gave the garden a '*zest de couleur*', she put aside her prejudices.

The curved paths in the *Jardin Italien* were a response to her husband's request for relief from the straight lines of the *potager*. This corner of the garden is shaded much of the day, allowing Cécile to experiment with subtle shades of colour and foliage which are a special interest. Limited by the climate, she tends to collect the same species and cultivars of families, such as the euphorbias and ivies which grow well there. Foliage is very important in Provence, because there are so few flowers between June and August, and the ornamental cabbages, artichokes and cardoons don't ripen until autumn. In the forecourt and rear terrace of the château she grows griselinia, hebe and veronica in Florentine jars, for their foliage only, removing the flowers.

THE RED DAHLIA STANDS OUT AGAINST A BACKGROUND OF COURGETTES, LAVENDER, AUBERGINES, SALVIA SCLAREA AND FENNEL. AKEBIA AND THE CLIMBING ROSE PAMPONETTE HUG THE WALL OF THE SHED.

RED HOT POKERS BOB IN THE FOREGROUND, GIANT CARDOONS RISE UP IN THE MIDDLE DISTANCE AND CYPRESSES REAR UP AGAINST THE BASTIDE OF VAL JOANIS.

In the *potager* she is looking increasingly for annuals with interesting foliage as part of a concerted effort to reduce the work on what is a very labour-intensive operation. A *potager à l'ancienne* represents an enormous amount of work, '*un travail épouvantable*', flowers and vegetables having different requirements in their care and cultivation. Cécile practises crop rotation and keeps a *carnet de plantations*. The perennials don't move, of course; the lavenders, rosemaries, mahonias, sage, box, artichokes, phitostegias, vitex and beuphorum. She gets carried away with different enthusiasms every year. Four years ago it was all green flowers in the *potager*; last year, cleome; and this year, argemone, a good substitute for the coveted romneyas, all the more desired because they are too tender to be grown here.

Surrounded as far as the eye can see by olive groves and vines, this working estate gives the *potager* a certain kudos. It is also extremely useful in many other ways, such as having a practically limitless supply of water, which is vital in running the vineyard. The *potager* runs on a *goutte à goutte* all night during the summer, and the rest of the garden is sprayed. The agricultural expert brought in to advise on care and treatment of the vines can also apply his expertise to the treatment of the hundreds of roses in the garden, because the rootstock of a rose is very similar to that of a vine. However, this is not the reason why roses are often seen planted at the end of each row of vines. The practice, explains Cécile (who has it on good authority from her husband), originated in Beaujolais and Bordeaux at a time when horses were used to pull the plough. Blindfolded to help them stay calm and walk in a straight line, they'd know, when they pricked their noses on the rose bush, that they had reached the end and must turn round. Nowadays, all these roses are modern polyantha roses, planted *pour faire chic*.

Cécile buys only French varieties of roses, as the English ones don't like the heat. At the end of July, she cuts all the flowers plus two or three leaves off all her roses, and after a little soil analysis applies a good dose of magnesium mixed with a little peat. They then rest for three weeks, only to flower even more profusely the next autumn.

The vineyard is also handy for compost. By law, all the grape skins and pulp must go to the local wine cooperative where the *eau-de-vie* is made. It is then bought back by the vineyard, aerated and mixed with peat, left for two years and finally used as a mulch. It improves the structure of the soil, allowing the nutrients to be absorbed more easily, and slightly lowers this astronomically high pH.

The policy of the vineyard has been to move increasingly towards an organic approach, and an expert is also brought in to advise on that. Previously, if red spider mite was spotted on a leaf, the whole vineyard would be sprayed automatically, which was both costly and ecologically destructive. Nowadays, only the vines in the parcel affected are sprayed, and the rest left alone. In the *potager* too, the fundamental organic principle of preventative gardening is practised, with disease-resistant varieties of flowers and vegetables being selected wherever possible. It is all hand weeded, and organic solutions are applied to pests and diseases, while organic fertilizers such as blood and bone are added, after tests made twice a year, to correct imbalances.

Ensconced in London during school terms and frequently travelling with her husband, Cécile does not have a lot of time left for cosseting temperamental plants. During the winter of 1985 she lost sixty per cent of the garden to frost, and vowed never again to introduce anything that wasn't hardy. Half-hardies have been known to slip on to the order form, but Cartesian logic prevails, and they are crossed out. She replaced her olive groves with hardier trees bought from a grove at an altitude of seven hundred metres, and so far all is well, but if these too should die, that's it! The five hundred litres of oil they produce annually is sold from the vineyard alongside their wines.

Living in England has given Cécile a perspective on both English and French gardens, and she helps herself to their ideas. The white garden at Sissinghurst has structure and informal planting, whereas Villandry she finds too formal, too flat. For the third year running she has opened Val Joanis under the French equivalent of the 'Garden Open Today' scheme, but no French visitor has ever asked a botanical question about the garden. The Italians think there are too many flowers; and only the English ever pose horticultural questions. If she lived at Val Joanis full time, she says, she would open a nursery with a good list of plants. So, if she could grow anything she wanted, what would it be? Everything Charles de Noailles did, of course!

They are now leaving a London house that has no garden, and have been looking for a house in Paris with a '*tout petit jardin*', but somehow have found one with a garden of nine hundred square metres. It's a dilemma. Gardens are like husbands, says Cécile – you can't have two at a time.

Chapter Five
BOTANICAL GARDENS

———— • ————

S O MUCH HAS BEEN MADE OF THE ENGLISH PRESENCE ON THE
Riviera, that it is often erroneously assumed that they introduced
most of the plants. However, one would be hard pressed to find
two more exciting botanical gardens than the Jardin Alpin du Lautaret
and the Jardin Exotique de Monte Carlo. The Riviera also has its great
collectors. Marnier Lapostolle, at Les Cèdres, with his bromeliads and
succulents, and Arpad Plesch, at Beaulieu, with his tropical fruits, are
both legendary names.

In fact, the botanical tradition on the Riviera goes back many centuries. As international trade increased, naval and botanical explorers
returned to southern French ports with plants from the East. They
began with a small botanical garden in Salon in 1762, created to acclimatize species brought back from the two Indies. Plants such as Cape
jasmine, Azores jasmine, Indian heliotrope and the Virginian tulip tree
came here before being sent on to the Jardin des Plantes in Paris.

The botanical garden in Toulon was created in 1786 for research into
medicinal plants – its proximity to the naval shipyard encouraged naval
officers to bring back seeds and plants for this purpose, from their
voyages. These were dispersed to interested gardens along the coast,
where, as the novelist Gustave Flaubert recorded: 'Under tall shady
trees, near a grassy bank, two or three convicts were at work in the garden; one could hear their chains dragging on the sand, but they had no
guard, no sergeant, no wardens.'

The history of the botanical garden of Marseilles is incredible; it was
established and dismantled in at least a dozen different locations.
Beginning stably enough six hundred years ago under the rule of Good
King René, around an elegant *bastide*, they innovatively grew carnations, new varieties of the muscat grape, and various fruit trees. After
that, it was all turbulence. In the sixteenth century, it became renowned as the place where a Colonel had executed his wife; in the
following century it was the pride and joy of the people of Marseilles,
and later the inspiration for an eighteenth-century poetess, who
wandered among the roses and figs. Numerous lemon trees sheltered in
huge glasshouses, and an ostrich amused the visitors with his gluttony.
Bought and rebought successively by local noblemen, it became in turn

HOME TO TROPICAL PLANTS,
THE PARC BORELY BOTANICAL
GARDEN IN MARSEILLES ALSO
BENEFITS FROM A LOCAL IRIS
GROWER'S DISCARDED
VARIETIES. ON THE LEFT, THE
MAUVE BACCARAT, ON THE
RIGHT IS DABBY RAINDON.
BEHIND IS A HUGE MASS OF
FLORIFERUS FELICIA
AMELLOIDES.

a library, a convent and an arsenal before eventually being made into a *jardin d'acclimatation* by Olivier de Serres, where he successfully grew Florentine pistachio trees, and was given two thousand plants from Empress Josephine, including species from Asia, Indonesia and America.

Its doors opened for the first time in 1817, with one hundred and twelve borders, four thousand species, and a huge rock garden created with plants brought from the Savoie. The fashionable crowds turned out on Sunday afternoons, dressed in their best, and were so inspired by the gardens that a botanical craze erupted, resulting in a hundred heated glasshouses being erected next to *bastides* all around Marseilles. Seeds and cutting were offered free to anyone who wanted them. Later, the garden disappeared under the railway line, and finally, in 1880, it settled on the site it occupies today. In 1900 the director of the garden, Dr Heckel, mounted a Colonial Pavilion at the Paris Exhibition. He also instigated numerous plant-hunting expeditions to the French colonies, produced a seed list, then broadened the scope of the garden by introducing what every Frenchman loves best – potentially edible plants such as gambo, yams, Japanese artichokes, the Uruguayan potato, and highly important disease-resistant vines from America.

The two world wars took their toll, and the gardens are now stable, but not exciting. Its nineteenth-century glasshouse, bought and erected in 1982, contains a permanent collection of orchids and tropical plants. The lovely irises on display are donated by a local iris breeder from his discontinued list – rather than throwing them out, he gives them to the garden. The primary aim now is to educate people to respect nature, by exposing them to a variety of tropical plants, climbers and perennials; parties of schoolchildren are taken round, to be shown what all the plants are, and where they come from. The younger children invariably like the banana trees best, and the drawings they send of their 'day out' are invariably of this tree. However, the bananas they draw are never their real colour, green, but always yellow, and usually hanging as an enormous solitary bunch, dwarfing the parent tree and all the other tropical plants. The children respond to what they can relate to and, unbelievably, most of the local children don't know what thyme is – even though it grows wild on the hills around them. Flowers don't grow on housing estates; bananas, one buys in a supermarket, and even thyme comes pre-packed from a shelf.

The palms, eucalyptus and mimosa – the flagships of the Riviera – were all imported and acclimatized, a process which has been described as breaking down a door already open. Generally, plants from tropical climates do not last – they tick over during the years with mild winters, and then are finished off by one hard winter. The best results have been obtained with sub-tropical plants from southern Australia, New South Wales, southern Africa, central Chile, central Argentina, Uruguay, and southern Brazil. Species from Arizona and California can also produce excellent results.

Botanical gardens – like all gardens – need inspired and visionary direction and a secure financial base from which to work. They too will have to prepare for the future by finding and experimenting with species of vegetation that are resistant to the effects of pollution, forest fires and erosion.

A CURVING LINE OF MME FERNANDEL IN THE FOREGROUND, RUSTICANA IN THE NEXT BED AND WAPITI AT THE END. ON THE HOOPS, ALBERTINE AND TALISMAN ARE THE MOST PROMINENT.

CHAPTER FIVE

Villa Thuret

GUSTAVE THURET

Born in 1817, in many ways, Gustave Thuret was similar to the Hanbury brothers. He came from a wealthy family, was socially and culturally well-connected – but was hounded out of France to Flanders for being Protestant. Thuret had already put aside a diplomatic career when he discovered a passion for marine algae, which would obsess him for the next thirty years. Searching in cold northern waters gave him rheumatism, and drove him south in 1855. He chose to live in Antibes, because the sea was rich in algae, and so became the first 'foreigner' to settle there. The Comté de Nice was still separate from France, whose frontier ended in the Var, and the railway only went as far as Cannes; beyond that, access was by a dirt road and stage-coach. Mimosas and eucalyptus were unheard of, the Cap being largely agricultural and relatively poor, and the Coin de Salisse, surrounding the hill on which Thuret established his garden, was still a swamp. When the locals saw him pulling out the vines and digging out the wheat to plant 'useless' things, they thought he was mad, and told him so – to this day the hill is known as *La Montée du Fou* (Madman's Hill) – not realizing that here was the goose which was about to lay the golden egg, by introducing horticulture to a region that had known only agriculture. The vast majority of plants now growing in gardens on the Riviera originated from trials held at the Villa Thuret. Even today, many potentially attractive or interesting species are introduced here with the aim of eventual assimilation into nurseries and garden centres across Europe.

In the beginning, it was difficult work. Gustave had to build his own house, part of it a laboratory, and water had to come from Antibes by mule. Worse still, he had no horticultural experience! Early results were disastrous: exposed in open fields, plants either froze in the winter or baked in the summer, and only when the Aleppo pines, the umbrella pines and holm oaks grew large enough to offer shade and protection from the sun and wind, could good results be obtained from the rich, acid soil. Through many diplomatic connections, Gustave was able, like the Hanburys, to obtain seeds and plant material from all the botanists – particularly Daniel Hanbury – who frequently came knocking on his door. The garden was laid out and planted in 1856, and has remained structurally unaltered since, although the villa has been completely rebuilt.

Thuret had been exceptionally successful with his identification of the sexual reproduction of algae – a remarkable achievement considering the quality of contemporary microscopes – and both he and his colleague, Dr Edouard Bornet, who analyzed the structure of lichens and experimented with hybridizing cistus, continued to triumph; but because they both hated writing, their findings weren't collated and published until 1910, just before Dr Bornet's death. Other sterling scientific results were obtained at the Villa by their successor Charles Naudin, whose research into heredity became the basis of Gregor Mendel's later work. Naudin brought the first *Jubea chilensis* to the garden and extended the eucalyptus collection. The garden is also noted for the palm, *Anorops richiena*, sent by Kew, of which only two examples exist in Europe, and the cycas collection – also very rare in Northern Europe.

The date palms *Phoenix dactylifera* were grown from date stones that were sown in 1861, but the fruits refuse to ripen, even in the mild southern climate.

When Gustave Thuret died in 1875, his sister-in-law gave the estate to the French government, stipulating that it must always be used as a scientific research institution. Altogether, fifty thousand species of plants have passed through the garden, and it addresses itself with authority to environmental, ecological and agronomical questions. Seven hundred species of trees have been tried out in designated arboretums throughout the Esterel, under deliberately harsh conditions, to try to replace dying species of vegetation unable to cope with present levels of pollution, or to identify those which could stop the growing problem of soil erosion – so far, fifty have been found to be potentially viable. Just as the landscape was once changed by the arrival of exotics, so it seems likely to change again with the effects of tourism and development. Working in horticulture, the Thuret staff are always looking – primarily amongst the Myrtaceae and Protaceae legumineuses – for original or exciting flowers and foliage to introduce to gardens via nurseries, sometimes from old species discovered in the archives. Seeds are planted out as young plants in the first or second year, depending on growth, and watered in summer only enough to keep them alive; in winter they are left unprotected. The garden is weeded, and the bases of the plants are hoed, but after that they are left to fend for themselves. It's the survival of the fittest; in this way they know which the fittest are likely to be. Four people look after the whole garden. Sometimes they are so short staffed that a specimen may not be labelled until it is fully grown, although the plants don't usually last that long. For, once they are established, the experiment is successful and therefore over – and something else is always waiting for the space. The nursery specialists come along and, if they approve, they ask for seeds or cuttings, which are freely given. A few years later, it may be available in a nursery. *Callistemon citrinus* and *fremontzia*, with its big yellow flowers, was introduced this way. 'It's difficult to know if it originates from here,' says Catherine Ducatillion, who runs the garden, 'but it doesn't matter. It is first and foremost a scientific garden. Entry is free, but it is not a park. The garden is like a shop window, where the displays have to keep up with the times.'

JARDIN ALPIN DU LAUTARET

GERARD CADEL

When Dr Tobias Smollett first came to the Côte d'Azur, he was so taken with the dazzling array of the wild flowers growing there that he described the whole area as 'mountains that are gardens'. The Jardin Alpin du Lautaret is just such a place. It was created in 1895 by a Professor Lachmann, professor of botany at the University of Grenoble, in one of the richest areas of natural flora in the Alps, and has had as

THE ROCKY MOUNTAIN RANGE IS ONE OF MANY REPRESENTED IN THE BOTANICAL ALPINE GARDEN OF THE LAUTARET.

many lives as the proverbial cat. It has survived two world wars, long periods of neglect, human tragedy, a chronic lack of funding, a hostile takeover bid and a relocation – and in spite of a rigorous climate it manages to grow two thousand alpine plants, including some of the world's rarest.

The garden has been steered through this obstacle course by a succession of intensely dedicated and dynamic professors, up to and including the present director, Professor Gerard Cadel, who hopes that the future of the garden is now secure. A witness to the garden's vicissitudes since his student days, he speaks from thirty years' experience when he says that 'in order to see an alpine garden live, you first have to see it die'.

Nearly thirty per cent of all the alpine flora species found in France grow in this pass which divides the northern and southern Alps. First discovered in the eighteenth century by one of the early alpine explorers, Dominique Villars, a botanist, doctor and priest from Grenoble, it was chosen by Professor Lachmann as the site for a small research station for the study and cultivation of alpine plants. It was laid out at the same time as Chamrousse, a second alpine garden much closer to the University and apparently more convenient. However, the eight-hundred-metre track leading from the road to the Chamrousse garden made access difficult, and it would have been too costly to improve it, so in the first of many twists of fate, Chamrousse was abandoned. The narrow bumpy road which left Grenoble and unravelled itself for ninety kilometres, climbing two thousand one hundred metres on its way to Lautaret, became the lifeline of the garden, but almost its hanging rope in 1912 when the Ministry of Transport decided to widen the road to bring in more tourists – and it seemed that their only 'attraction' would be swallowed up in the process. Instead, the University, the Touring Club de France and the Paris-Lyon-Mediterranean railway agreed to move the garden; and the whole thing was transplanted to another site, fifty metres higher, chosen for its breathtaking view – but whose hundred and thirty mile per hour winds also eroded most of the topsoil. It was no accident that in 1911 Captain Scott used this location to test his equipment prior to the fateful expedition to the South Pole – winter temperatures combined with the Col's ferocious winds created conditions closely resembling those of the Antarctic. At the top of the garden there is a commemorative plaque to Scott and his men on a cairn erected by the Touring Club de France. The garden was purposely relocated next to an hotel also owned by the PLM railway, in the hope of attracting clients, and the gardener was fed and housed here, tending the hotel *potager* as well as the alpine garden.

The new garden was officially opened after the First World War in 1919, and enjoyed a period of splendour until 1939. By now the Jardin Alpin had far exceeded the budget of a small laboratory, and the University had agreed to take it on. By the time war broke out, it comprised the most comprehensive collection of alpines growing anywhere in the European Alps, with three or four thousand species, under the able direction of Monsieur Prével, who became active in the French Resistance. During the Liberation in 1944 the Germans, as a parting reprisal, took the men in the area hostage, including Monsieur Prével and the proprietor of the hotel, and shot them dead in a nearby tunnel; a chapel commemorates them. After this tragic death the garden was abandoned – its chalet and buildings were occupied by retreating troops, and eventually nothing was left of the chalet but an empty shell. The fence around the garden had also been destroyed, so sheep devoured virtually everything; and what they didn't eat, plant enthusiasts dug up.

The garden lay in ruins until 1950, when two more professors stepped in: Madame Kofler, who restored the chalet and fencing, and Monsieur Ruffier-Lanche, a self-taught enthusiast who was well known in English gardening circles. Together they rebuilt the collection from two hundred to more than five thousand species, but in the process overstretched themselves: for a garden of five thousand species requires prodigious labour, and to keep introducing new plants without 'reinforcements' was a sure-fire recipe for disaster. A garden, after all, is a completely artificial environment where existing species are removed and new ones introduced. The indigenous plants ask for nothing better than to reoccupy their former home, and within a matter of a few years, they can quite easily destroy an alpine garden.

HERACLEUM RISES DRAMATICALLY AGAINST AN EQUALLY IMPRESSIVE ALPINE BACKDROP WHICH INCLUDES THE PEAK COMBEYNOT SEEN IN THE DIP ON THE RIGHT.

The garden began a slow decline around 1965, accelerated by the death there of Ruffier-Lanche's daughter – a shock from which her father never recovered – and in 1973 he too died; but there were no memorials this time, and no benefactors. The garden fell into the neglectful hands of an indifferent successor, so that by 1981 ninety per cent of the collection had vanished, leaving all but the most robust plants choked by weeds and other indigenous plants. Expensive to re-store, vulnerable to predators, it had become an enormous financial liability to the University of Grenoble, which was looking for a way out. Meanwhile the Parc National des Ecrins was hovering in the side-lines, wanting to buy it. A political and pragmatic approach was needed if it was going to be saved. At this point a saviour turned up in the form of Gerard Cadel. He knew that, for all the promises made by the Parc National des Ecrins, their real intention was to trivialize the garden by having a tiny botanical corner with a hundred indigenous plants along-side huge rockeries of bedding to make a splash for the tourists. 'I had never thought it was my destiny to become the director of a botanical garden,' said Cadel, but he stepped in.

Gerard Cadel is first and foremost an ecologist; a vigorous 'defender' of nature. He knew the garden well, having stayed in its chalet many times from 1960 onwards, studying the dry conditions of the neigh-bouring Brianconnais forest, and at the same time observed the problems inherent, specific and unique to an alpine garden. Under the maxim that you can only protect well what you know well he saw in this garden a unique opportunity to introduce the general public to alpine flora, which they would normally never see – certainly not against such an impressive backdrop – and in so doing make them aware of the need to protect their environments all over the globe.

The only way to prevent the University selling the garden to the Parc des Ecrins was to make the garden self-supporting. Cadel hired a young man, Monsieur Lestani, who knew very little about alpine plants but was a very good gardener. Cadel was to train him botanically and between 1983 and 1987 the two of them blitzed the whole garden, while still managing to keep it open. Twenty new rockeries were added, and the layout was transformed, so that the Parc des Ecrins no longer wanted either to pay the increased value or to put it all back as it was. Having thwarted the 'takeover bid', Cadel set up a charity which would manage the garden financially and charge an entrance fee – something which the University was not allowed to do.

The garden itself looks a little like a relief map. There are now ninety rockeries, covering five acres, grouped by origin and theme. Half of them are devoted to alpine flora, and the rest represent most of the higher mountain ranges of the world, including the Pyrenees, the Rockies, the Himalayas, and the Caucasian and Siberian ranges. There are also areas of alpine meadow. The position was well chosen to dazzle the tourist, but it does create problems: in summer the winds sweep most of the humus from the topsoil, leaving the tender plants exposed to scorching heat. Had the garden been situated three or four hundred metres lower, all those local plants that grow around Briançon could have been included: a whole subspecies of alpine flora which cannot survive at the present altitude; and if were not so directly exposed to the sun – even if it were north facing – a yet wider range of plants could

THE PEAK LA MEIJE RISING ON THE LEFT OVERLOOKS A ROCKERY OF ICELAND POPPIES, EUPHORBIA HYBERNA, PRIMULA AURICULATA, CALTHA PALUSTRIS, AND RENUNCULUS ACONITIFOLIUS.

be displayed. The garden is only open for ten weeks from late June because early snows arrive during September and the pass may be closed to traffic. By the beginning of October the head gardener must have everything tidy and be ready to leave at a moment's notice. Twenty years ago, they were caught out early in September and had to be evacuated with sledges and dogs.

Visitors often ask whether the plants are brought in during the winter, but it is in fact the blanket of snow which normally protects them. Come May, the discrepancy between day and night temperatures is enormous. If there is no snow as a shield against the sunshine, the heat wakes the plant up, making the sap rise, and leaving it at the mercy of night frost. Deciding where to plant what – locating the micro climates within the garden – is very difficult, as it is not always known which areas will be favoured by snow and how long it can be counted on to remain. Moving a plant one metre may make all the difference.

Soil conditions are slightly acid, which suits most plants – even lovers of lime, most of which manage. Sometimes a bit of rock calcaire is added to give carbonate of calcium. For a long time no fertilizer at all was applied, but now they use a little. Because of its exposure to blasting wind, the soil and its nutrients are constantly being blown away and replenished with peat with a little fertilizer.

The most successful of the mountain ranges represented in the garden are those with similar climates – where the summer is very dry. Plants from the Pyrenees do better here than elsewhere in the Alps, and the Caucasian mountains are well represented. Especially successful are plants from America's Rocky mountains, such as penstemon and phlox. They thrive because they like the climate, but Professor Cadel's team have had difficulty with ranges which are more humid, such as the eastern Himalayas (the Sikim), and the Japanese, and Arctic ranges. In trying to redesign the Arctic rockery a system is being devised whereby the plants are constantly supplied with water, as in the Arctic habitat itself. The garden was marginally enlarged to conserve tufaceous rocks, formed by underground water courses passing through limestone gradually resembling pumice stone with cavities, which are widespread in the region. They are an excellent growing medium because of their sponge-like structure. The rockeries are weeded three times a year; first and most importantly at the beginning of the season; a task which is completed as quickly as possible. The second weeding follows two weeks later, and the last is done late in the season, to make the spring weeding easier by ensuring that nothing has had a chance to become established the previous autumn. Volunteers help to make new rockeries and to 'overhaul' the old ones, which need rethinking, dividing, replacing, removing.

When Monsieur Lestani, the head gardener, beats a hasty retreat from his alpine hideout at the first signs of snow, he will have put the garden to bed and collected the seed for his index seminum, a list which is sent to three hundred other botanical gardens with substantial alpine collections. While waiting for those gardens to send their own lists, he can take his annual holiday. Then, as the other gardens' seed lists arrive, he and Cadel look for plants which would be interesting to try, because the garden considers itself as a museum in growing and propagating certain rare plants to preserve them. Seeds which have been collected from plants growing in the wild are preferable to those from a cultivated source because it ensures genetic purity. It is also important to know how reliable the source is. As a general rule, the older the garden's curator, the more experienced he will be, and the more certain one can be of getting the right plants, and healthy seeds. Very few people can correctly identify all the alpine flora, even after thirty years, and correctly identifying and labelling all the plants during the garden's salvage operation was a big headache. The Jardin Alpin presents its public with a very detailed plant list few other gardens are able to offer. 'We can't just amuse ourselves,' says Cadel, 'by ordering thousands of seeds and having ninety per cent fail, so we order around five or six thousand species, and in the spring we sow them in the little greenhouse lab at the University in Grenoble. Twelve years ago the success rate was thirty per cent; today, because we know the ecology of what we order and how to grow them, we have a seventy per cent success rate – which apparently is very high for alpine plants. When you visit an alpine garden, go straight to the greenhouse, and from the state of the nursery you'll be able to assess the health of the garden. An alpine garden in full swing has a very good nursery, and if there isn't one it means the garden is dying. It generally takes seven years before a plant grown from seed is ready to be planted out into the rockery. They need to mature in conditions that are less difficult than those outside, otherwise you couldn't introduce these alpines into the garden.'

THE MIDDLE EAST AND SIBERIAN ROCKERIES SEEN WITH THE SNOW-COVERED LA MEIJE IN THE BACKGROUND. SEEN HERE ARE DIANTHUS MONSPESSULANUS, GERANIUM IBERICUM, YELLOW PAPAVER NUDICALE AND ORANGE PAPAVER LATERITIUM.

HISTORY AND EXOTICISM MIX
IN THE VIEW OF THE GRIMALDI
CASTLE FROM THE JARDIN
EXOTIQUE DE MONACO.

JARDIN EXOTIQUE DE MONACO

MARCEL KROENLEIN

In 1863 in an effort to raise money for the principality Charles III, great-grandfather of Prince Rainier, commissioned a casino modelled on the successful money-spinner in Bad Hamburg. Erected on a giant piece of rock overlooking the sea, with a few olive trees and goats, it was named Monte Carlo – after Charles. Although gambling was illegal in neighbouring France, business was still diabolical. The croupiers would loaf about, and every so often look through a telescope in search of clientele, before going back to the tables. One of those early croupiers was Valentin Kroenlein. Eventually prosperity arrived, as the railway was extended from Nice, and the casino prospered. This enabled Charles's son Albert to commission the Jardin Exotique, as well as an Oceanography Museum. The success of the casino also established the Kroenlein family in Monaco, and Valentin's grandson was to make the Exotic Garden almost as famous as the casino.

The Jardin Exotique de Monaco was born almost by accident, and certainly by coincidence. One of Monaco's municipal gardeners, Augustin Gastaud, had begun collecting succulents, which he laid out in beds near to the construction site of the new Oceanography Museum. These strange and noble plants attracted the attention of Prince Albert, an amateur naturalist, who often passed when overseeing his Museum but who had never seen such succulents and cacti

152

before. He called in the municipal engineer Louis Notari, noted for his architectural and aesthetic expertise, to consider the creation of a permanent exhibition, whose hanging gardens would later become almost as famous as those in that other earlier Babylon. It is now the most photographed spot on the Côte d'Azur, and only the Oceanography Museum has more visitors.

Lying on a curve of the Moyenne Corniche, and sharing the same latitude as New York and Vladivostok, Monte Carlo enjoys temperatures between 12 and 24°C; the driest, hottest, stillest spot was found – the most perfect microclimate on the coast. The site is screened from north winds and cold breezes by Mont Angel and Tête du Chien, and favourably exposed to east winds which bring rain, and west winds bringing sunshine.

As if the precipitous drop of the cliff face was not impressive enough, huge artificial hollow 'rocks', fabricated from steel mesh and concrete, were positioned in the garden, giving it an extra dimension and perspective – and enormous scope for planting. Around these vast boulders, bridges were built, vaults constructed and belvederes suspended, adding character to the overhanging walls and sheer rock faces. The whole was interwoven with a labyrinthine network of paths – a remarkable feat of architecture and engineering which took twenty years to complete.

Marcel Kroenlein joined the garden in 1954 and was made director in 1969. His interest in cacti and succulents stems from an early fascination with all plants that struggle to live and which few people understand. This is analogous to the work of his ancestors in the desert of what is now Namibia, who tried to decipher the 'clicking' language of the bushmen. After leaving the Ecole National Supérieure d'Horticulture in Versailles, he went to the Jardin Alpin du Lautaret to study the response of alpine plants to the harsh, dry conditions of the mountains. Alpines have only three months to grow and reproduce before the first snows enforce their winter dormancy, but the problems encountered in a barren desert are greater still. From Lautaret he came directly to the Jardin Exotique, but would have preferred to work in a national park because of his passion for both flora and fauna; had the garden existed for tourist purposes only, he would not have stayed, but the scope for expansion was enormous.

CEREUS PERUVIANUS, ONE OF MANY STARS IN THE COLLECTION.

Although open to the public since 1933, the garden had no collections of any importance, and these he has made his life's work. Having learned from the ups and downs of the Jardin Alpin, Dr Kroenlein has developed and promoted the Jardin Exotique, quadrupling admissions to six hundred thousand, which has financed his many plant-hunting safaris. He has personally contributed over two thousand plants. Now one of the world's experts, he has recently written the definitive encyclopaedia on succulent plants and cacti.

The Jardin now owns and houses a staggering collection of euphorbias, aloes, ferocactus and mammillaries, gymnocalysium and pilosocereus,

among the twenty families of plants culled from all over the world. They come from botanical institutions and cacti buffs. The search for rare succulents and cacti takes Marcel himself to the desert regions of the southern USA, Mexico, South America, Africa, Madagascar, the Yemen and many other countries.

The Riviera is not a frost-free paradise, it does have marked climatic extremes. People tend to think of cacti and succulents as plants from hot climates, but in fact they are xerophytes, which means plants from dry countries: as long as they remain dry they can withstand severe subzero temperatures. In very cold weather the plants are covered with strong cloth and then plastic to repel moisture. The winter of 1985 brought temperatures of -5°F, which for this garden is like Siberia. The giant African euphorbias, which follow their natural cycle of winter growth, can be protected up to a height of four metres, but when they reach eight, it is no longer possible, and they die. 'We pulse them with hot air, but it's *au revoir*. Fortunately they grow very quickly.' Kept dry, opuntias have been known to survive -45°F – but not in Monte Carlo! Although 800mm of rain falls on Monaco, the steep garden slopes sixty metres, so the rain runs off, good drainage, of course, is crucial.

Care of plants is often tricky: very tall specimens have to be tethered to stop them toppling over and breaking in the wind; and for weeding on the steep cliffs the gardeners have to wear a parachute harness. Every three years, the top three inches of soil is replaced; every seven, the soil mixture changed completely. In the meantime each plant is con-

stantly monitored, and the observations are recorded. The Jardin Exotique is represented at numerous flower shows and exhibitions. A single specimen weighing as much as a ton has to be packed and loaded on to trucks alongside others of every prickly shape and size. It is a very delicate manoeuvre, and one slip could be fatal – for both the plant and the handler. Another incident requiring a degree in engineering concerned a specimen in the glasshouse which had grown to forty feet and was about to burst through the roof. It had to be dug up and replanted in a large hole excavated two metres deeper.

Across the Moyenne Corniche, opposite the garden, are the greenhouses, closed to the general public, which house the permanent botanical collections. Here, rare species are preserved, plants propagated to replace those lost, and students trained. This is also where the distribution of seeds or cuttings of rare plants takes place, as well as the highly detailed indexing of those which are constantly arriving from a worldwide network of fellow enthusiasts, scientists and educational institutions.

Increasingly pressed for space, Marcel sometimes goes cap in hand to his friend Prince Rainier to ask for a few extra feet on which to erect a nursery. It is not inconceivable that he may have expropriated the French of a yard or two soil. The financial and botanical stability of this garden is due to the dynamism, enthusiasm and expertise of its director. Without Marcel Kroenlein the only way to maintain the standard would be to break the bank at Monte Carlo.

A JUNGLE OF CACTI AND SUCCULENTS GATHERED FROM ALL OVER THE GLOBE DAZZLE THE VISITOR. THIS EXOTIC GARDEN WAS CARVED OUT OF THE CLIFF FACE.

GARDENS OPEN *to the* PUBLIC

Gardens in this list look good at any time of year, although March, April, May, June, September and October are the most exhuberant months. Oranges and lemons are on the trees throughout the winter.

ITALIAN RIVIERA

LA MORTOLA
CAPE MORTOLA, VENTIMIGLIA
TEL: 010 39 184 229507
WINTER HOURS: FROM 1 OCTOBER 10-4.
GATES CLOSE AT 5PM. GARDEN CLOSED
WEDNESDAYS.
SUMMER HOURS: FROM 1 JUNE OPEN DAILY
9-6. GATES CLOSE AT 6PM.
GUIDED VISITS BY APPOINTMENT.

BOCCANEGRA
LATTE, VENTIMIGLIA
CONTACT GUIDO PIACENZA AT HIS
NURSERY, THE MINI ARBORETUM, BIELLA,
13057 POLLONE, ITALY. TEL: 010 39 15 61693
THE NURSERY CARRIES OLD FASHIONED
ROSES AND AN INTERESTING LIST OF
PLANTS. OPENING HOURS 9-12.30 AND 2.30-
6.30.
BOTANICAL GROUPS MAY VISIT THE GARDEN
BY APPOINTMENT.

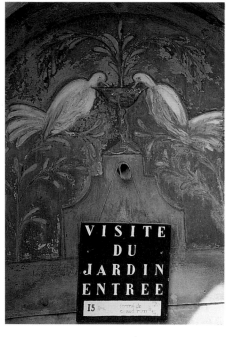

LES COLOMBIÈRES

FRENCH RIVIERA
MENTON AND MONACO AREA

JARDIN EXOTIQUE DE MONACO
62 BLVD DU JARDIN EXOTIQUE
98002 MONTE CARLO
OPEN DAILY: JANUARY 9-5.30; FEBRUARY
AND MARCH 9-6; APRIL 9-6.30; MAY, JUNE,
JULY, AUGUST 9-7; SEPTEMBER 9-6.30;
OCTOBER 9-6; NOVEMBER 9-5.30; DECEMBER
9-5.

VAL RAHMEH BOTANICAL GARDEN
MUSEUM OF NATURAL HISTORY
AVENUA ST JACQUES
06500 MENTON
TEL: 010 33 93 35 86 72
WINTER HOURS: FROM 1 OCTOBER 10-12 AND
2-5.
SUMMER HOURS: FROM 1 MAY 10-12 AND 5-6.
HALF PRICE ADMISSION FOR GROUPS OF
MORE THAN 25.

SERRE DE LA MADONE
ROUTE DE GORBIO
06500 MENTON
VISITS BY WRITTEN REQUEST TO THE
OWNER:
MADAME ROSE GREDIG
57 RUE GRIMALDI
MONACO
TEL: 010 33 93 50 28 17
ENTRY IS GRATIS AT PRESENT.

LES COLOMBIÈRES
ROUTE DES COLOMBIÈRES
TEL: 010 33 93 35 71 90
GUIDED VISIT OF HOUSE AND GARDEN 20
FRANCS; CHILDREN UNDER 12 FREE.
REDUCED RATE FOR GROUPS.

FONTANA ROSA
6 AVENUE BLASCO IBAÑEZ
06500 MENTON
VISITS BY WRITTEN REQUEST TO: JEAN
HUBERT GILSON
MAIRIE DE MENTON, BP 69
06502 MENTON CEDEX

VILLA MARIA SERENA
21 PROMENADE REINE ASTRID
06500 MENTON
COLLECTION OF TROPICAL PLANTS.
OPEN TUESDAYS FROM 10AM.
ENTRANCE 30 FRANCS; 500 FRANCS FOR
GROUPS OF 20 TO 50 PEOPLE.

PARC DU PIAN, MENTON
AVENUE BLASCO IBAÑEZ
OVER FIVE HUNDRED ANCIENT OLIVES.

PALAIS CARNOLES, MENTON
AVENUE DE LA MADONE
CITRUS COLLECTION.
MADAME JOSIANE TRICOTTI ORGANISES
GUIDED VISITS AROUND MENTON'S PUBLIC
GARDENS ON BEHALF OF THE MAIRIE.
TEL: 010 33 92 10 33 66.

AROUND GRASSE

VILLA NOAILLES
59 BLVD GUY DE MAUPASSANT
06130 GRASSE
TEL: 010 33 93 36 07 77
OPEN EVERY FRIDAY. GUIDED VISITS 10.30
AND 2.30.

L'OUSTAOU DEÏ BAÏLEA
CHEMIN DU PARADIS CHEMIN DU BOSQUET
06620 BAR SUR LOUP
TEL: 010 33 93 42 55 17
VISITS BY APPOINTMENT WITH BRUNO
GORIS AND DAILY IN JUNE. OLD ROSE
NURSERY.

ILE DE FRANCE – MUSÉE ROTHSCHILD
BLVD EPHRUSSI DE ROTHSCHILD
06230 ST JEAN CAP FERRAT
TEL: 010 33 93 01 33 39
OPEN 1 NOVEMBER TO 15 FEBRUARY 10-5 ON
WEEKENDS, PUBLIC HOLIDAYS AND SCHOOL
HOLIDAYS. FROM FEBRUARY 15 OPEN 10-6.

VILLA THURET
BOULEVARD DU CAP D'ANTIBES
06605 CAP D'ANTIBES
TEL: 010 33 93 67 88 66
INTERESTING TO BOTANISTS.

LES COLLETTES

HAUT DE CAGNES
06800 CAGNES SUR MER
TEL: 010 33 93 20 61 07
AUGUSTE RENOIR'S GARDEN.
CLOSED EVERY TUESDAY AND FROM MID-
OCTOBER TO MID-NOVEMBER.
OPEN FROM 1 MAY TO MID-OCTOBER 10-12
AND 2-6; FROM MID-NOVEMBER TO 30 APRIL
10-12 AND 2-5.

CHÂTEAU DE GOURDON

06620 BAR SUR LOUP
OPEN FROM 1 OCTOBER 2-6, CLOSED
TUESDAYS; DAILY FROM 1 JUNE 11-1 AND 2-7.

JARDIN EXOTIQUE EZE

RUE DU CHATEAU
06620 EZE
PUBLIC PARK OPEN 9-12 AND FROM 2 TO
DUSK.

HYÈRES

The gardens of Edith Wharton and
Charles de Noailles are of easy walking
distance apart and both are well sign-
posted. Parc St Bernard is an exciting
garden in its own right with a good collection of Mediterranean plants. Exhibitions
are held in the house.

PARC ST BERNARD

TEL: 010 33 94 35 90 00
OPEN FROM DAWN TILL DUSK.

CASTEL STE CLAIRE

OPEN FROM DAWN TILL DUSK.
PUBLIC GARDEN

ILE DE FRANCE

MARSEILLES

BOTANICAL GARDEN OF MARSEILLES

PARC BORELY
62 AVENUE CLOT BEY
13272 MARSEILLES
TEL: 010 33 91 55 25 02 62
GOOD FOR IRISES AND ROSES; TROPICAL
PLANTS ARE KEPT IN THE GREENHOUSE.

CHÂTEAU D'ANSOUIS

84240 ANSOUIS
TEL: 010 33 90 09 82 70
OPEN DAILY FROM EASTER TO END
OCTOBER 2.30-6. CLOSED ON TUESDAYS
DURING THE WINTER. THE GARDEN IS OPEN
TO GROUPS DAILY BY APPOINTMENT.

CHÂTEAU DE ROUSSAN

ROUTE DE TARASCON
13210 ST REMY DE PROVENCE
OPEN AS A HOTEL.
TEL: 010 33 90 92 11 63

OTHER GARDENS/PLACES OF INTEREST RECOMMENDED BY AUTHOR

CHÂTEAU D'ENTRECASTEAUX

83 ENTRECASTEAUX, VAR
BEAUTIFULLY RESTORED CASTLE OFTEN
HOUSES ART AND PHOTOGRAPHY
EXHIBITIONS. SHOP.
TEL: 010 33 94 04 43 95

ABBAYE ST ANDRE

RUE MONTÉE DU FORT
FORT ST ANDRE
30400 VILLENEUVE LES AVIGNON
TEL: 010 33 90 25 55 95

ABBAYE DE SENANQUE

NEAR GORDES
FRAGRANT ROWS OF LAVENDER.

ABBAYE ST ANDRE

THE ARRIÈRE PAYS AND PROVENCE

JARDIN ALPIN DU LAUTARET

05220 MONETIER LES BAINS
TEL: 010 33 76 51 46 00
OPEN DAILY FROM 25 JUNE TO 8 SEPTEMBER
10-6.30.
ENTRANCE 20 FRANCS, CONCESSIONS 14
FRANCS.
GUIDED VISITS ON WRITTEN REQUEST TO
THE GARDEN.
SPECTACULAR SETTING.

CHÂTEAU VAL JOANIS

84120 PERTUIS
VISITS ALL YEAR BY APPOINTMENT WITH
CATHERINE CHANCEL.
TEL: 010 33 90 79 20 77
VINEYARD AND POTAGER. BUY THE WINE,
SMELL THE FLOWERS!

ABBAYE DE SENANQUE

INDEX

Page numbers in **bold** type refer to illustrations and their captions.

BIBLIOGRAPHY

Michael J. Arlen, *Exiles*, Andre Deutsch 1971
Martin Bailey, *Vincent Van Gogh – Letters from Provence*, Collins & Brown 1990
Consuelo Vanderbilt Balsan, *The Glitter and the Gold*, William Heinemann 1953
Alfred H. Barr, Jr *Matisse – His Art and His Public*, Museum of Modern Art, New York 1951
James Henry Bennet, *Winter and Spring on the Shores of the Mediterranean*
Arnold Bennett, *The Journals*, Penguin 1971
Mary Blume, *Côte d'Azur: Inventing the French Riviera*, Thames and Hudson 1992
Lord Henry Brougham *Life and Times*
Jane Brown, *Eminent Gardeners*, Viking 1990
Christian Byk, *Guide des Jardins de Provence et de Côte d'Azur*, Berger-Levrault/Nice Matin 1988
Robert Calder, *Willie – The Life of W. Somerset Maugham*, William Heinemann 1989
Philip Callow, *Van Gogh – A Life*, W. H. Allen 1991
Roderick Cameron, *The Golden Riviera*, Weidenfeld and Nicholson 1975
Leslie de Charms, *Elizabeth of the German Garden*, William Heinemann 1958
Kenneth Clark, *Another Part of the Wood*, John Murray 1974
Ethne Clarke, *Hidcote – The Making of a Garden*, Michael Joseph 1990
Colette, *La Naissance du Jour*, G.F. Flammarion 1928
Colette, *Prisons et Paradis*, Fayard 1986
Cyril Connolly, *The Rock Pool*, Oxford University Press 1981
Jean Paul Crespelle *Guide de la France Impressioniste*, Hazan 1990
E. C. Cripps, D. Chapman-Huston, *Through a City Archway: The story of Allen & Hanburys*, John Murray 1954
E. C. Cripps, *Plough Court: The story of a notable pharmacy*, Allen & Hanburys 1927
Honoria Murphy Donnelly with Richard N. Billings, *Sara and Gerald, Villa America and After*, Times Books 1982
John Dos Passos, *The Best Times*, Andre Deutsch 1968
John Dos Passos, *The Fourteenth Chronicle*, Andre Deutsch 1974
Derek Fell, *Renoir's Garden*, Frances Lincoln 1991
G. T. Garratt, *Lord Brougham*, Macmillan and Co. 1935
Marcel Gaucher, *Les Jardins de la Fortune*, Hermé 1985
Martin Gilbert *Never Despair, Winston S. Churchill 1945-1965*, Minerva 1988
Marcel Haedrich *Coco Chanel; Her Life, Her Secrets*
Dorothy Hanbury, *La Mortola Garden*, Oxford University Press 1938
Augustus Hare, *The Years with Mother*
Augustus J C Hare *The Rivieras*, George Allen 1897
A. Hill, *Henry Nicholson Ellacombe*
Patrick Howarth, *When the Riviera was Ours*, Century 1977
Collingwood Ingram, *A Garden of Memories*, H. F. & G. Witherby Ltd 1970

Louisa Jones, *Gardens in Provence*, Flammarion 1992
Frances Kennett, *Coco: The Lives and Loves of Gabrielle Chanel*, Gollancz, New York 1965
Marcel Kroenlein, *Exotic Garden*, Edizioni Kina Italia
Roy Lancaster and Charles de Noailles, *Mediterranean Plants and Gardens*, Floraisse 1974
Audrey Le Lievre, *Miss Willmott of Warley Place*, Faber and Faber 1980
R. W. B. Lewis, *Edith Wharton – A Biography*, Harper and Row 1975
R.W.B. and Nancy Lewis, *The Letters of Edith Wharton*, Simon and Schuster 1988
Herbert Lottman, *Colette – A Life*, Minerva 1991
Alex Madsen, *Coco Chanel*, Bloomsbury 1990
Katherine Mansfield, *Letters and Journals*, Penguin 1977
W. Somerset Maugham, *Strictly Personal*, William Heinemann 1942
Elsa Maxwell, *The Celebrity Circus*, W.H. Allen 1964
Ted Morgan, *Somerset Maugham*, Johnathan Cape 1980
Harold Nicholson, *Diaries and Letters 1930-39*, Collins 1966
David Ottewill, *The Edwardian Garden*, Yale University 1989
Dorothy Parker, *What Fresh Hell is This?*, Heinemann 1988
Robert Phelphs, *Belles Saisons – A Colette Scrapbook*, Farrar, Straus and Giroux 1978
Michel Racine, J.P. Boursier-Mougenot, *Gardens of Provence and the French Riviera*, Edisud 1987
Charles Quest Ritson, *The English Garden Abroad*, Viking 1992
Jean Renoir, *Renoir My Father*, The Reprint Society Ltd 1964
Evelyne Reymond, *Colette et la Côte d'Azur*, Edisud 1988
Edmonde Charles-Roux, *Chanel*, Johnathan Cape 1974
Meryle Secrest, *Kenneth Clark*, Weidenfeld and Nicholson 1984
Mary Soames, *Clementine Churchill*, Penguin 1981
Mary Soames, *Winston Churchill – His Life as a Painter*, Collins 1990
Tobias Smollett, *Travels through France and Italy*, Oxford University Press 1979
Robert Louis Stevenson *Letters*
Robert Stewart, *Henry Brougham 1778-1868*, Bodley Head 1986
David Sweetman, *The Love of Many Things – A Life of Vincent Van Gogh*, Hodder and Stoughton 1990
Calvin Tomkins, *Living Well is the Best Revenge*, Andre Deutsch 1972
G. Tweedale, *At the Sign of the Plough*, John Murray 1990
Karen Usborne, *'Elizabeth'*, Bodley Head, 1986
Edith Wharton, *A Backward Glance*, Charles Scribner's Sons 1933
Edith Wharton, *Italian Villas and Their Gardens*, Century Co 1904
Derek Wilson, *Rothschild*, Andre Deutsch 1988